Massachusetts Bucket List Adventure Guide

Explore 100 Offbeat Destinations You Must Visit!

Erin Briggs

Canyon Press
canyon@purplelink.org

Please consider writing a review!
Just visit: purplelink.org/review

ISBN: 978-1-957590-12-7

FREE BONUS

Discover 31 Incredible Places You Can
Visit Next! Just Go To:

purplelink.org/travel

Table of Contents:

How to Use This Book

Welcome to your very own adventure guide to exploring the many wonders of the Commonwealth of Massachusetts. Not only does this book lay out the most wonderful places to visit and sights to see in the vast state, but it provides driving directions and GPS coordinates for Google Maps to make exploring that much easier.

Adventure Guide

Sorted by region, this guide offers over 100 amazing wonders found in Massachusetts for you to go see and explore. These can be visited in any order, and this book will help keep track of where you've been and where to look forward to going next. Each portion describes the area or place, what to look for, Physical Address, and what you may need to bring along.

GPS Coordinates

As you can imagine, not all of the locations in this book have a physical address. Fortunately, some of our listed wonders are either located within a National Park or Reserve or are near a city, town, or place of business. For those that are not associated with a specific location, it is easiest to map it using GPS coordinates.

Luckily, Google has a system of codes that converts the coordinates into pin-drop locations that Google Maps can interpret and navigate.

Each adventure in this guide will include both the GPS coordinates along with general directions on how to find the location.

It is important that you are prepared for poor cell signals. It is recommended to route your location and ensure that the directions are accessible offline. Depending on your device and the distance of some locations, you may need to travel with a backup battery source.

About Massachusetts

The Commonwealth of Massachusetts is one of the most historic states in the country. Its first English settlers came to the area in 1620 on the *Mayflower*. Their settlement in Plymouth was the second permanent colony established in what would eventually become the United States.

Massachusetts played a critical role in the American Revolution. Many events surrounding the rebellion against British rule originated in Boston. This state was one of the original 13 colonies in the formation of the United States and officially became the country's sixth state on February 6, 1788.

Massachusetts has since grown into one of the most prominent states in the country. The state was a major hub for abolitionist activity before the Civil War and is now the home of many of the country's top schools, including Harvard, MIT, Northeastern, Boston College, Amherst College, and Tufts.

Landscape and Climate

With an area of about 10,500 square miles, Massachusetts is the country's seventh-smallest state. The western part of the state features the northern end of the Appalachian Mountains, while the central part is a hilly area. The eastern region is a coastal plain that covers Cape Cod and the Boston area.

Most of the central and western areas of Massachusetts are in a humid continental climate. The Boston region is in a humid subtropical climate, while Cape Cod has an oceanic climate. The summers in Massachusetts are warm, with highs in the 80s for much of the season. Temperatures typically drop below freezing throughout the winter. Coastal temperatures are typically cooler in the summer and warmer in the winter.

The commonwealth is subject to nor'easters during the winter. These storms can bring hurricane-force winds and heavy amounts of rain or snow.

According to the 2020 census, Massachusetts ranked in the top third of the country by population, with about 7 million residents. Nearly 5 million of them live in the Boston metropolitan area, making it the tenth-largest area in the country. Other prominent cities in Massachusetts include Springfield, Worcester, Lowell, Salem, New Bedford, and Fall River.

About 20 percent of the people living in Massachusetts are of Irish descent. The Wampanoag Tribe has two reservations in eastern Massachusetts, while the Nipmuc tribe has two in the central part.

Massachusetts is bordered by every other state in New England except for Maine. Interstate 95 goes through the eastern end of the state and links to Rhode Island and Portland, Maine. The Massachusetts Turnpike (I-90) stretches more than 130 miles from Boston to the western end of the state, going through Worcester and Springfield along the way. The Massachusetts Bay Transportation Authority operates many of the public transportation services in the commonwealth.

The commonwealth has more than a hundred higher education centers. Harvard University and the Massachusetts Institute of Technology are both in

Cambridge. Boston University has the largest enrollment, with more than 30,000 students attending classes every year. The University of Massachusetts campuses in Amherst, Lowell, and Boston are the largest public schools in the state.

Most of the professional sports teams in the state are based in the Boston area. The city of Boston is home to the Celtics, Bruins, and Red Sox basketball, ice hockey, and baseball teams. The nearby town of Foxborough is home to the New England Patriots football team and the New England Revolution soccer club.

Emily Dickinson Museum

The Emily Dickinson Museum in Amherst is actually two buildings. The first is the Homestead, where Emily Dickinson was born in 1830 and where she lived from 1855 to her death in 1886. Her bedroom is on full display here. The room is believed to be where she wrote most of her poems. Many of her works were discovered here after her death.

The Evergreens home is the other building at the museum site. This house was built for Emily's brother Austin and his wife, Susan. It has been refurbished to look as it did when they lived there. Many of the features in the house might have helped influence some of Emily's many poems.

Best Time to Visit: The museum is very popular around December 10, Dickinson's birthday.

Pass/Permit/Fees: Admission is $15 for adults and $10 for children.

Closest City or Town: Amherst

Physical Address:
Amherst College
280 Main St
Amherst, MA 01002

GPS Coordinates: 42.37610° N, 72.51452° W

Did You Know? Emily Dickinson and other members of her family are buried about half a mile north of the museum in the Amherst West Cemetery.

Eric Carle Museum of Picture Book Art

This museum in Amherst focuses on the art of children's picture books. The museum was founded by children's book author and illustrator Eric Carle.

The museum showcases the unique designs of various children's picture books and how they have evolved. Some of the drawings on display include work by Leo Lionni, Chris Van Allsburg, Maurice Sendak, and Dorothy Kunhardt. The museum also has original art pieces from various Golden Books.

Best Time to Visit: The museum hosts various exhibitions highlighting work by Carle or other artists and trends and concepts in picture books. Visit the museum's details on what exhibits are currently on display.

Pass/Permit/Fees: Admission to the museum is $9.

Closest City or Town: Amherst

Physical Address:
The Eric Carle Museum of Picture Book Art
125 W Bay Rd
Amherst, MA 01002

GPS Coordinates: 42.32108° N, 72.53319° W

Did You Know? Eric Carle's picture books have sold more than 50 million copies, and his work has been translated into more than 60 languages.

Aquinnah Cliffs

The western end of Martha's Vineyard is home to the Aquinnah Cliffs overlook, which is surrounded by the Atlantic Ocean. The Gay Head Lighthouse is visible in the middle part of the area.

The cliffs are made of red clay that has built up over millions of years. The water around the beach is often colored red because of the eroding clay from the cliffs. Moshup Beach is also nearby.

Best Time to Visit: The sunset hours are the most popular time to visit because the landscape is beautiful at this point in the day.

Pass/Permit/Fees: It is free to get to the cliffs.

Closest City or Town: Aquinnah

Physical Address:
Aquinnah Cliffs Overlook
31 Aquinnah Cir
Aquinnah, MA 02535

GPS Coordinates: 41.34776° N, 70.83830° W

Did You Know? The nearby lighthouse was moved more than 100 feet inland in 2015 because of worries about its stability. The seas around the area have become increasingly powerful in recent years.

Doane's Falls

This is a 175-foot chain of wide cascades and plunges on a 46-acre preserve managed by the Trustees of Reservation. There are three easy-to-distinguish sections. The first section is a pair of plunges set against a stone-bridge backdrop. When you follow a well-marked trail downstream, you will discover the next two sections of Doane's Falls. After passing several cascades, you will reach a 20-foot block waterfall streaming over a ledge. This is Lawrence Brook, a tributary of the Millers River, which continues with small cascades and pools, eventually dumping into Tully Lake. Visitors are asked to stay on the trail because there has been substantial erosion over the years. This water is dangerous, so it is completely off-limits for swimming, wading, and whitewater kayaking.

Best Time to Visit: The waterfalls are open year-round for hiking and fishing.

Pass/Permit/Fees: The area is free to visit.

Closest City or Town: Athol

Physical Address:
Doane's Falls / Tully Lake Trailhead
Doane Hill Rd
Royalston, MA 01368

GPS Coordinates: 42.64871° N, 72.20170° W

Did You Know? The waterfall is part of an engineering project designed to keep floodwaters under control in the local region.

Beacon Hill and the Black Heritage Trail

The Beacon Hill neighborhood of Boston is home to the Massachusetts State House. The area is famous for its many sites related to Black history in the city. You can tour these sites by walking the Black Heritage Trail.

The Black Heritage Trail includes many sites that date to before the Civil War. The African Meeting House is the country's oldest African-American church building. The Abiel Smith School and the residences of abolitionists John Coburn and George Middleton are among the sites on the trail.

Best Time to Visit: The trail is open throughout the year.

Pass/Permit/Fees: There is no free to walk the trail, but admission may be required for some of the sites here.

Closest City or Town: Boston

Physical Address:
Black Heritage Trail
46 Joy St
Boston, MA 02114

GPS Coordinates: 42.35810° N, 71.06277° W

Did You Know? In 1783, Massachusetts was the first state in the country to make slavery illegal, which eventually made Beacon Hill a popular site for escaped slaves to live.

Boston Common and Public Garden

Boston Common is a public park in the southern part of Boston. The 50-acre park features multiple walking paths and monuments, including the Soldiers and Sailors Monument and the Boston Massacre Monuments.

The Public Garden is immediately west of Boston Common. Established in 1837, this 24-acre park was the country's first public botanical garden. Don't miss the massive equestrian statue of George Washington on the western end.

The swan boats are popular attractions that take people around the entire perimeter of the lake inside the garden.

Best Time to Visit: The swan boats are open from April to August every year.

Pass/Permit/Fees: It costs $4.50 for adults and $3 for children to board one of the swan boats.

Closest City or Town: Boston

Physical Address:
Public Garden
4 Charles St
Boston, MA 02116

GPS Coordinates: 42.35416° N, 71.06963° W

Did You Know? Boston Common has a monument dedicated to the Oneida Football Club, the first organized football club in the United States. The club played there from 1862 to 1865.

Boston Harbor Islands State Park

You will find 34 small islands off the coast in the Boston Harbor Islands State Park. Many of these islands are open for touring and can be reached by ferry.

Spectacle Island features a beach and several picnic sites. Georges Island houses Fort Warren, an old Civil War-era base. Little Brewster Island is home to the Boston Light, which is the oldest lighthouse in the country, constructed in 1716.

Best Time to Visit: The summer season is the best time to visit because the waters will be calmer.

Pass/Permit/Fees: The cost to board a ferry to reach any of these islands varies by charter service.

Closest City or Town: Boston

Physical Address:
Boston Harbor Islands State Park
191 W Atlantic Ave
Boston, MA 02109

GPS Coordinates: 42.31722° N, 70.95374° W

Did You Know? Free ferry services are available between some of the islands. These include ferries that go between the Georges and Spectacle islands. Private boats can also dock on some, although reservations may be required for certain spots.

Boston Harbor Walk and Christopher Columbus Waterfront Park

Boston's Harborwalk is a path that surrounds the shoreline and other features around Boston Harbor. The walkway goes from East Boston to Columbia Point and leads to attractions such as the New England Aquarium, Bunker Hill Monument, and the Kennedy Presidential Library. Christopher Columbus Waterfront Park is one of the most popular sites on the Boston Harborwalk. The park is home to the Rose Kennedy Rose Garden, a memorial dedicated to the Americans killed in the 1983 attack on a barracks building in Beirut.

Best Time to Visit: You can travel down the Boston Harborwalk and visit the park at any time of the year, although the conditions are nicer in the summer.

Pass/Permit/Fees: Access to the area is free, but it may cost money to rent a bicycle for traveling down the walkway.

Closest City or Town: Boston

Physical Address:
Christopher Columbus Waterfront Park
Atlantic Ave
Boston, MA 02110

GPS Coordinates: 42.36103° N, 71.05165° W

Did You Know? There were efforts to expand the Boston Harborwalk to include some spots near the Logan Airport, but those plans were abandoned.

Boston Harbor Whale Watching

Boston Harbor, located on the eastern end of Boston, is the western extension of Massachusetts Bay. The main docks on the harbor are near the end of the waterfront neighborhood; many of them are close to Christopher Columbus Waterfront Park.

The harbor is a popular launching site for whale-watching tours that start here and head out to the open waters. People can see whales migrating to the area during the summer season or observe when they are migrating south in the winter.

Best Time to Visit: The summer and fall seasons are the best times to visit the harbor and see whales.

Pass/Permit/Fees: The cost of a whale-watching tour varies. Expect to spend about $50 per person.

Closest City or Town: Boston

Physical Address:
Boston Harbor City Cruises
1 Long Wharf
Boston, MA 02210

GPS Coordinates: 42.36051° N, 71.04983° W

Did You Know? Whales often arrive in Massachusetts during the summer season because of the high levels of krill and plankton in the water.

Boston Public Library and Copley Square

The Boston Public Library's main building in Copley Square is one of the most historic libraries in the country. Originally opened in a former two-room schoolhouse in 1854, it moved to a new building in 1858 and into its present location in 1895. The Renaissance-style building features an array of murals painted by John Singer Sargent.

Public tours are available throughout the year. The building has a vast array of sections around its five floors. The library also houses a few dining spots, including the Courtyard Tea Room, which serves one of Boston's largest selections of loose-leaf teas.

Best Time to Visit: The library is open Monday through Saturday.

Pass/Permit/Fees: The library is free to visit or tour, but food prices vary by location.

Closest City or Town: Boston

Physical Address:
Boston Public Library – Central Library
700 Boylston St
Boston, MA 02116

GPS Coordinates: 42.34931° N, 71.07815° W

Did You Know? The library is in the middle of Copley Place, a shopping area that links to the Prudential Center complex.

Boston Tea Party Ships & Museum

Learn about the Boston Tea Party of 1773 at the Boston Tea Party Ships & Museum complex. The museum houses full-scale replicas of several of the ships that took part in this essential part of American history.

You'll see what the ships looked like and learn how the events of the Boston Tea Party unfolded. The museum has a performance theater and a small tea café.

This attraction teaches people about the importance of the Boston Tea Party and how it helped lead to the American Revolution. The panoramic theater here screens films about how this event led to many future actions opposing British rule.

Best Time to Visit: The museum is open Thursday through Monday.

Pass/Permit/Fees: Tickets are $29.95 for adults and $21.95 for children.

Closest City or Town: Boston

Physical Address:
Boston Tea Party Ships & Museum
306 Congress St
Boston, MA 02210

GPS Coordinates: 42.35224° N, 71.05123° W

Did You Know? The Robinson Tea Chest is the most prominent artifact at the museum. The tea chest is the only known surviving chest from the Boston Tea Party.

Cocoanut Grove Memorial

The Cocoanut Grove Memorial in Boston's Bay Village neighborhood is at the former location of the Cocoanut Grove nightclub, the site of one of the deadliest fires in American history. The fire took the lives of 492 people on November 28, 1942.

The memorial displays a floor plan of the Cocoanut Grove and explains how the event led to many changes to fire codes throughout the country. Overcrowding in the building, various flammable surroundings, and locked exit doors led to the massive death toll.

Best Time to Visit: The memorial is open to visit at any time.

Pass/Permit/Fees: The memorial is free to reach.

Closest City or Town: Boston

Physical Address:
Cocoanut Grove Memorial Plaque
1-13 Piedmont St
Boston, MA 02116

GPS Coordinates: 42.35004° N, 71.06784° W

Did You Know? The Lund and Browder Chart was developed based on experiences from treating victims of the Cocoanut Grove fire. The chart is still used today because it helps doctors estimate the total body surface area impacted by a burn. The system makes it easier for burn victims to be treated.

Faneuil Hall

Faneuil Hall is a public market near Boston's Waterfront district. The hall was built in 1742 as a public market house. It has been used for many governmental events and speeches, but it now functions mainly as a shopping destination. With more than 200,000 square feet of retail areas and 160,000 square feet of other space, Boston's iconic mixed-use festival marketplace is home to more than 70 retailers. Visitors can also indulge in a variety of cuisines at its restaurants and pubs and in the world-famous Quincy Market Colonnade. World-renowned street performers and musicians entertain on the cobblestone promenades.

Best Time to Visit: The Christmas season is a popular time to visit the hall because the place is decked out in various festive décor. The hall also hosts a few pop-up stores.

Pass/Permit/Fees: Prices for products at all the shops and dining spots around Faneuil Hall will vary.

Closest City or Town: Boston

Physical Address:
Faneuil Hall Marketplace
4 S Market St
Boston, MA 02109

GPS Coordinates: 42.36026° N, 71.05467° W

Did You Know? Ted Kennedy, John Kerry, and Mitt Romney are among the various Massachusetts government officials who have made major speeches at Faneuil Hall over the years.

Fenway Park

Fenway Park, the oldest active park in major league baseball, has been the home of the Boston Red Sox since 1912. It has a capacity of approximately 37,000 fans.

The park features a unique field design, which includes a right-field foul pole at an unusual angle and a triangle-shaped extension in the centerfield area.

The Green Monster wall in left field is about 37 feet high. The venue hosts various other events throughout the year, including concerts, football games, and even outdoor ice hockey events.

Best Time to Visit: Tours are available throughout the year, but their availability varies depending on what events are taking place at the ballpark.

Pass/Permit/Fees: Tours of Fenway Park are $21 for adults and $15 for children.

Closest City or Town: Boston

Physical Address:
Fenway Park
4 Jersey St
Boston, MA 02215

GPS Coordinates: 42.34675° N, 71.09742° W

Did You Know? The Boston Braves also played at Fenway Park from 1914 to 1915. The team played elsewhere in Boston after that and eventually moved to Milwaukee and then Atlanta, where they play today.

20

Freedom Trail

The Freedom Trail is a 2.5-mile walk through Boston that leads to 16 important sites in American history. The trail is easy to follow because it's marked by a colored-brick path.

The trail includes spots at Boston Common, the Massachusetts State House, the USS *Constitution*, Paul Revere's house, and the grounds of Boston Latin School. The site of the Boston Massacre and King's Chapel, with its adjacent burial ground, are also on the trail.

Best Time to Visit: The Freedom Trail is open year-round, but it is especially popular on Independence Day and other patriotic holidays.

Pass/Permit/Fees: An official tour from the Freedom Trail Foundation costs $14 for adults and $8 for children.

Closest City or Town: Boston

Physical Address:
Freedom Trail Starting Point
Boston Common
Boston, MA 02108

GPS Coordinates: 42.36638° N, 71.05473° W

Did You Know? The National Park Service is in charge of some of the activities on the Freedom Trail. The NPS has an office on the first floor of Faneuil Hall.

Isabella Stewart Gardner Museum

The Isabella Stewart Gardner Museum in Boston is housed inside a complex designed to look like a Venetian mansion. The museum has thousands of paintings, books, and other items collected from many eras of art history worldwide, including works by Titian, Dante, Botticelli, and Matisse.

The museum has an archives department containing thousands of letters from many correspondents. These include letters from Oliver Wendell Holmes, T.S. Eliot, and numerous other people who communicated with Gardner during the creation of the museum.

Best Time to Visit: The museum hosts various exhibitions throughout the year. You can visit the Gardner Museum website to learn about the latest events.

Pass/Permit/Fees: Admission is $20 for adults and $13 for students.

Closest City or Town: Boston

Physical Address:
Isabella Stewart Gardner Museum
25 Evans Way
Boston, MA 02115

GPS Coordinates: 42.33823° N, 71.09881° W

Did You Know? The museum has a few empty frames for some of the paintings that were stolen in a 1990 theft. The 13 works that were stolen have yet to be recovered.

John F. Kennedy Presidential Library and Museum

The John F. Kennedy Presidential Library and Museum is devoted to the life and work of the 35th President of the United States. The museum has exhibits on Kennedy's involvement in the Civil Rights Movement and the Space Race.

 You will find the Freedom 7 capsule that was flown by Alan Shephard in 1961 and a replica of the Resolute desk used in the Oval Office at the museum. Many pieces of First Lady Jacqueline Kennedy's wardrobe are on display, as well as a 25-foot sailboat owned by the Kennedy family.

Best Time to Visit: The museum is open on weekends. People are encouraged to book reservations to visit.

Pass/Permit/Fees: Admission is $14 for adults and $10 for children.

Closest City or Town: Boston

Physical Address:
University of Massachusetts Boston
Columbia Point
Boston, MA 02125

GPS Coordinates: 42.31626° N, 71.03419° W

Did You Know? The library also has a collection of items from Ernest Hemingway. The writer's widow has a strong relationship with the Kennedy family.

Logan International Airport 9/11 Memorial

The Logan International Airport in Boston is home to a memorial dedicated to the victims of the two flights involved in the terrorist attacks of September 11, 2001, that originated from Boston. The memorial is a 20-foot-by-20-foot glass cube in a park space outside the airport.

Two glass rectangles inside are etched with the names of the people on American Flight 11 and United Flight 175, the two Boston-based flights that were flown into New York's World Trade Center. Other pieces of glass hanging from the ceiling shimmer in the sun. The building is surrounded by a cluster of trees on top of a small hill. Two curved walkways loop toward the cube. It is said that they reflect the paths taken by the two hijacked planes.

Best Time to Visit: The memorial is open 24 hours a day.

Pass/Permit/Fees: The memorial is free to visit.

Closest City or Town: Boston

Physical Address:
Terminal A
1 Harborside Dr
Boston, MA 02128

GPS Coordinates: 42.36628° N, 71.02258° W

Did You Know? Large American flags fly outside of Gates B32 and C19, the two gates where the flights took off.

Make Way for Ducklings Statue

One of the most popular features in Boston's Public Garden is the *Make Way for Ducklings* statue. The statue was built in 1987 as a tribute to the children's book of the same name, written by Boston resident Robert McCloskey.

The statue takes up about 35 feet of the northeastern part of the Public Garden. Mother Mallard takes the lead with her eight ducklings—Jack, Kack, Lack, Mack, Nack, Ouack, Pack, and Quack—following her on a cobblestone path.

Best Time to Visit: The ducks are often decorated for various holidays and special occasions throughout the year.

Pass/Permit/Fees: The statues are open throughout the day.

Closest City or Town: Boston

Physical Address:
Public Garden
4 Charles St S
Boston, MA 02116

GPS Coordinates: 42.35552° N, 71.06977° W

Did You Know? The book *Make Way for Ducklings*, which takes place in the Boston Public Garden, has been continuously published since it was introduced in 1941.

MIT Museum

This museum is owned and operated by the Massachusetts Institute of Technology, one of the country's most prominent schools. The museum has a massive collection of more than 1 million objects, prints, rare books, technical archives, drawings, photographs, and films. Items range from MIT's founding in 1861 to current cutting-edge research, including more than 25,000 object records from the Hart Nautical Collections. It also has the world's largest hologram collection, with hundreds of hologram products on display. The MIT Museum has a few kinetic art pieces as well. These are pieces that the viewer will perceive as moving based on motions or angle of view.

Best Time to Visit: The Cambridge Science Festival occurs every April at the MIT Museum. The festival hosts many special science exhibits and projects.

Pass/Permit/Fees: Admission is $10 for adults and $5 for children.

Closest City or Town: Boston

Physical Address:
MIT Museum
265 Massachusetts Ave Building N51
Cambridge, MA 02139

GPS Coordinates: 42.36319° N, 71.08285° W

Did You Know? Some of the displays at the museum include MIT student pranks from over the years. One of them is a drinking fountain designed to look like it was directly connected to a fire hydrant.

Museum of Fine Arts, Boston

The Museum of Fine Arts in Boston is one of the world's largest art museums in terms of area. The museum has more than 300,000 items in its collection, including artifacts from Ancient Egypt and the Dutch Golden Age. Many French Impressionist paintings and Chinese calligraphy works are also on display. The museum has the world's largest collection of Japanese art outside of Japan. There are more than 5,000 Japanese ceramic works and 4,000 paintings in its collection. The museum is guarded on the outside by Cyrus Dallin's *Appeal to the Great Spirit* statue. It is the fourth of Dallin's Epic of the Indian statues.

Best Time to Visit: The museum hosts different exhibitions from around the world, which you can learn about on the museum's website. The website has the latest schedule of exhibitions.

Pass/Permit/Fees: Admission to the museum is $25 per person.

Closest City or Town: Boston

Physical Address:
Museum of Fine Arts, Boston
465 Huntington Ave
Boston, MA 02115

GPS Coordinates: 42.33957° N, 71.09398° W

Did You Know? Gilbert Stuart's unfinished 1796 portrait of George Washington is on display at the museum. The painting is considered to be the inspiration for the design on the one-dollar bill.

Museum of Science

Boston's Museum of Science, located on the Charles River in the Science Park area, offers many exhibits throughout its three wings. The Red Wing has an animal care center, a planetarium, and a large-screen theater. The Green Wing has an indoor bird habitat and an exhibit highlighting human sciences.

The Blue Wing houses an exhibit on dinosaurs, a theater dedicated to understanding electricity and how it works, and an indoor garden where live insects and many native plants can be found.

Best Time to Visit: The museum is popular on weekends when there are many live animal sessions.

Pass/Permit/Fees: Admission is $29 for adults and $24 for children.

Closest City or Town: Boston

Physical Address:
Museum of Science
1 Museum of Science Driveway
Boston, MA 02114

GPS Coordinates: 42.36766° N, 71.07141° W

Did You Know? The dinosaur exhibit is highlighted by a full-size *Tyrannosaurus rex* model.

New England Aquarium

Explore the amazing marine world of New England at the New England Aquarium, located at the Central Wharf in Boston. The aquarium has nearly 600 species of marine life on display.

The Giant Ocean Tank is the largest tank at the aquarium. It features a coral reef design and includes sea turtles, stingrays, barracuda, and bonnethead sharks. There is also a vast penguin habitat at the aquarium that includes southern rockhopper and African penguins.

Other segments include a harbor-seal exhibit and a tropical-fish tank. A tide pool exhibit includes hermit crabs and many other New England–based animals.

Best Time to Visit: The aquarium is open all year.

Pass/Permit/Fees: Admission is $10 for adults and $8 for children.

Closest City or Town: Boston

Physical Address:
New England Aquarium
1 Central Wharf
Boston, MA 02110

GPS Coordinates: 42.35921° N, 71.04934° W

Did You Know? The Giant Ocean Tank holds about 200,000 gallons of water.

North Point Park

The 8.5-acre North Point Park opened in downtown Boston in 2007. It is on the Charles River near the Craigie Drawbridge. The venue includes multiple islands with a few pedestrian walkways connecting them. One of these islands is shaped like a circle.

The park has a playground with a splash pad open on the mainland. The area offers many places for children to enjoy wading. Some of the walkways at the park also go near the waterway.

Best Time to Visit: The water-based activities here are open during the summer months.

Pass/Permit/Fees: The park is free to visit.

Closest City or Town: Boston

Physical Address:
North Point Park
6 Museum Way
Cambridge, MA 02141

GPS Coordinates: 42.36925° N, 71.06898° W

Did You Know? The park was created primarily to replace old parkland spaces that were dug up during the Big Dig, a project that entailed producing several tunnels for I-90 and I-93. The Big Dig was designed to reduce traffic congestion in the Boston area, but it has been controversial for its high budget and impact on parks.

Old North Church and Boston's North End

Boston's North End neighborhood has been inhabited by Europeans since at least the 1630s. It includes such historical sites as Paul Revere's house and the Copp's Hill burial ground.

The Old North Church is one of the most historic sites in North End. From here, signals were sent to warn people in Boston of the impending arrival of British forces. The event was critical to Revere's midnight ride on April 18, 1775. The church has been in operation since 1723, and most of its Georgian structure remains intact today.

Best Time to Visit: The church is open for Mass on weekends.

Pass/Permit/Fees: The church is free to visit.

Closest City or Town: Boston

Physical Address:
Old North Church
193 Salem St
Boston, MA 02113

GPS Coordinates: 42.36634° N, 71.05438° W

Did You Know? There are about a thousand bodies buried in the crypt underneath the church. The crypt, which was used from 1732 to 1860, contains the bodies of some soldiers who died at the Battle of Bunker Hill.

Skinny House of Boston

The Skinny House of Boston is a unique "spite house" that is 10.4 feet wide and 9.25 feet deep. A spite house is an unusual property built to obstruct various buildings, usually out of defiance or anger toward another party. The property was constructed in the 1870s on 44 Hull Street in Boston's North End district.

The home was built after one brother in a family was given very little land to build on, and much of his inheritance was lost. He was unhappy about his other brother building a large home that took up most of the space, so he built Skinny House to block the sunlight from reaching the larger building.

Best Time to Visit: You can go by the house any time of the year.

Pass/Permit/Fees: You can only look at the home from the outside because it's a private residence that sold for $1.25 million in September 2021.

Closest City or Town: Boston

Physical Address:
Skinny House
46 Hull St
Boston, MA 02113

GPS Coordinates: 42.36690° N, 71.05624° W

Did You Know? The building is four stories high and has five doors and multiple stairwells.

Spectacle Island

Spectacle Island is a 114-acre island about 4 miles east of Boston. It features a small beach, 5 miles of trails, and a marina. There are no paved roads on the island. Its walking paths are maintained by the city because it is part of the Boston Harbor Islands National Recreation Area.

This was once two small drumlins connected by a narrow spit, which looked like a pair of spectacles (hence the name). Much of the island was resurfaced in the 2000s. Dirt and clay dug up during Boston's Big Dig project were utilized to help resurface the island and prepare its many walking paths and recreational sites. Thousands of trees were planted, and paths, buildings, and a dock were built.

Best Time to Visit: It is easier to access Spectacle Island during the summer months because ferries head to the island more often during that season.

Pass/Permit/Fees: It costs $25 for a round-trip ferry ride to reach the island.

Closest City or Town: Boston

Physical Address:
Spectacle Island Visitors Center
82C7+R3
Quincy, MA 02171

GPS Coordinates: 42.32404° N, 70.98616° W

Did You Know? Spectacle Island opened to the public in June 2006 as a recreational area with hiking trails, a beach, a visitors' center, and café, and a marina.

Stellwagen Bank National Marine Sanctuary

The Stellwagen Bank National Marine Sanctuary is a marine habitat in the Massachusetts Bay between Cape Cod and Cape Ann. The area is popular for its whale-watching tours. Visitors can see many whales here, including the sperm, beluga, orca, and pilot whales. Other ocean animals that might be spotted include common and bottlenose dolphins, gray and harp seals, and the great white shark.

Best Time to Visit: Most trips to the sanctuary are from May to October. The water is easier to manage then, and migrating whales will often be seen in the waters during these months.

Pass/Permit/Fees: Check with a boat charter in the Boston area for details on how you can reach the sanctuary. Some charge at least $50 per person for a trip to the area by boat.

Closest City or Town: Boston

Physical Address:
7 Seas Whale Watch (one of many charter options)
63 Rogers Street
7 Seas Wharf
Gloucester MA 01930

GPS Coordinates: 42.46209° N, 70.33410° W

Did You Know? Stellwagen Bank is not a financial bank but an underwater plateau in the local area named for Commander Henry Stellwagen of the U.S. Navy.

USS Constitution Museum

The USS Constitution Museum at Boston's Navy Yard is home to the famous ship that was launched in 1797 and served during the War of 1812. The museum illustrates how "Old Ironsides" was built and how sailors lived at sea on the heavy frigate.

The museum includes a look at the War of 1812, including how it started and what happened. The story of the battle between the USS *Constitution* and the HMS *Java* is illustrated here.

Best Time to Visit: The museum is open all year, but the ship may be closed during inclement weather.

Pass/Permit/Fees: Admission is $15 for adults and $10 for children.

Closest City or Town: Boston

Physical Address:
USS Constitution Museum
Building 22, Charlestown Navy Yard
Charlestown, MA 02129

GPS Coordinates: 42.37406° N, 71.05546° W

Did You Know? The USS *Constitution* is the oldest U.S. Navy ship still in active service. It last sailed in 2012 in honor of the 200th anniversary of her defeat of the HMS *Guerriere*.

Warren Anatomical Museum

The Warren Anatomical Museum on the Harvard Medical School campus in Boston houses many specimens and artifacts relating to medical history, including items collected in the nineteenth century by Dr. John Collins Warren, a prominent surgeon.

The museum features many unique medical appliances that were used during that time period. Among them are a tabletop sterilizer, children's crutches, and an ether inhaler used for surgical anesthesia. The most notable artifact here is the skull of Phineas Gage, which has a massive puncture wound in the top where an iron rod went through his brain and skull, an injury that Gage survived.

Best Time to Visit: The museum is open year-round. The array of artifacts on display will vary throughout the year.

Pass/Permit/Fees: Admission is free, but an appointment is recommended.

Closest City or Town: Boston

Physical Address:
Francis A. Countway Library of Medicine
10 Shattuck St
Boston, MA 02115

GPS Coordinates: 42.33526° N, 71.10363° W

Did You Know? There are nearly 15,000 items in the museum's collection. There are a few living specimens, but they are off-limits to the public.

Cape Cod Museum of Natural History

This museum has a 17,000-square-foot building on 80 acres abutting an additional 320 acres of town and conservation land. The combined land includes a wide range of habitats: pitch pine woodlands, salt marshes, a barrier beach, and beech forests. The building houses exhibits about the area's natural history and archeology, including a butterfly house, some beehives, a small aquarium, and collections of stuffed and wooden birds. The Marshview Room offers a view of conservation lands with binoculars for birdwatching and a monitor displaying a live stream of the osprey nest in the marsh.

Best Time to Visit: The museum is open Monday and Wednesday from 8 a.m. to 4 p.m.; Tuesday and Thursday from 9 a.m. to 2 p.m.; Fri from 8 a.m. to 3 p.m.; Saturday from 8 a.m. to 6 p.m.; and Sunday from 9 a.m. to 4 p.m.

Pass/Permit/Fees: Admission is $12 for guests over age 12, $5 for children ages 3–12, and free for children under age 3.

Closest City or Town: Brewster

Physical Address:
Cape Cod Museum of Natural History
869 Main Street/Route 6A
Brewster, MA 02631

GPS Coordinates: 41.7544° N, 70.1158° W

Did You Know? Stony Brook, the small river that courses through the nearby land, is a herring run during the spring.

American Repertory Theater

The American Repertory Theater (ART) on the Harvard University campus in Cambridge hosts various musical and play productions throughout the year. The ART focuses on experimentation and going beyond the traditional boundaries of theater performance.

Most of the programs at the ART are premieres of new plays and musicals. The theater provides an opportunity for theater enthusiasts to train and develop their skills in performance and production. Many of the productions here have earned prominent awards such as the Pulitzer Prize and the Tony Award.

Best Time to Visit: The ART has a full schedule of theatrical performances throughout the year. Visit the theater's website to learn more about what's playing here.

Pass/Permit/Fees: Ticket prices vary by program.

Closest City or Town: Cambridge

Physical Address:
Loeb Drama Center
64 Battle St
Cambridge, MA 02138

GPS Coordinates: 42.37487° N, 71.12296° W

Did You Know? The Loeb Drama Center is the main building at the ART. The center has room for about 500 people for each show.

Charles Riverboat Company

Enjoy a cruise on the Charles River and along Boston Harbor on a boat provided by the Charles Riverboat Company. The boat company operates in Boston's East Cambridge neighborhood. The riverboat company offers sightseeing tours that show you many of the unique buildings and historical sites throughout Boston. It also has architectural tours that take you through many unusual sites. Evening cocktail cruises are also available.

Best Time to Visit: The fall is the company's most popular time for cruises. You can book a seat on one of the fall foliage cruises and see the trees as they change colors for the season.

Pass/Permit/Fees: Ticket prices vary by event. A traditional sightseeing cruise costs $23 for adults and $14 for children. Tickets are available two weeks before a scheduled departure, so try to book your reservations in advance.

Closest City or Town: Cambridge

Physical Address:
Charles Riverboat Company
100 Cambridgeside Pl
Cambridge, MA 02141

GPS Coordinates: 42.36880° N, 71.07608° W

Did You Know? A typical cruise is about 70 minutes long and will take you past many of the universities in the area, including Harvard and MIT.

Fresh Pond Reservation

You will find many walking trails and paths to explore on the Fresh Pond Reservation in Cambridge. The reservation surrounds Fresh Pond and includes trails that go around the entire body of the pond.

The reservation is home to a public golf course, a children's play area, and a butterfly meadow. A few small wooded spaces are around the reservation area. In addition to a wide variety of resident birds, many migrating songbirds and waterfowl pass through every year.

Best Time to Visit: The park is open throughout the year, but the trails around the area are easier to travel down during the summer and fall seasons.

Pass/Permit/Fees: While you can visit the reservation for free, you need a permit if you're going to use the area for an event or activity involving at least 25 people.

Closest City or Town: Cambridge

Physical Address:
Fresh Pond Reservation
250 Fresh Pond Pkwy
Cambridge, MA 02138

GPS Coordinates: 42.38285° N, 71.14401° W

Did You Know? You can walk your dog down many of the trails around the reservation. Leashes may not be required, but it depends on whether your dog will respond to whatever commands you issue.

Harvard Art Museums

There are three museums in the Harvard Art Museums complex east of Harvard Yard. These museums contain approximately 250,000 objects. The Fogg Museum hosts many Dutch Master, Flemish Renaissance, and French Baroque paintings. The collection includes works from van Gogh, Titian, Gauguin, and Monet.

The Busch-Reisinger Museum focuses on art from German-speaking countries in Europe. The Arthur Sackler Museum has a collection of Asian art pieces and artifacts, including Chinese jade items, Buddhist temple sculptures, and Japanese paper art. Mediterranean and Islamic art pieces are also on display at the Sackler Museum.

Best Time to Visit: The museums' host events throughout the year. Visit the Harvard Art Museums' website to see what events are coming.

Pass/Permit/Fees: Admission is $20 for adults. Children under age 18 are admitted free of charge. Some special exhibitions may cost extra, so check the website for details.

Closest City or Town: Cambridge

Physical Address:
Harvard Art Museums
32 Quincy St
Cambridge, MA 02138

GPS Coordinates: 42.37411° N, 71.11429° W

Did You Know? The Fogg Museum was formed in 1895, making it the oldest museum on the Harvard campus.

Harvard Museum of Natural History

The Harvard Museum of Natural History is on the university's campus in Cambridge. It houses exhibits about animals from all over the world. You will see mounted specimens of many animals from Africa and Asia, including Siberian and Bengal tigers.

The glass flowers are the most popular items. The museum has 4,300 glass models of plants representing 780 species. The flowers are made with real glass materials, some with paint used on their bodies. Wire supports reinforce a few internal spots in these flowers. Other displays here include *Rockefeller Beetles*, a display showing hundreds of beetle specimens.

Best Time to Visit: The museum hosts many special events and public lectures throughout the year. For the schedule of events, check the Harvard website.

Pass/Permit/Fees: Admission is $15 for adults and $10 for children.

Closest City or Town: Cambridge

Physical Address:
The Harvard Museum of Natural History
26 Oxford St
Cambridge, MA 02138

GPS Coordinates: 42.37849° N, 71.11561° W

Did You Know? Some of the glass flowers on display include simulated looks at the effect of blight and rot on various plants, including fruits.

Harvard Square

Harvard Square is a business district in the historic center of Cambridge adjacent to Harvard Yard. More than 8 million people visit every year to shop, dine, browse bookstores, visit coffeehouses, hear folk music and street performers, and view public art.

The district features many Colonial Revival and Greek Revival buildings throughout the area, and many monuments dedicated to the Revolutionary War can be seen.

The square also hosts numerous public events relating to Harvard University, including rallies before sporting events.

Best Time to Visit: The square may be the easiest to visit during the summer months when the university isn't hosting as many classes.

Pass/Permit/Fees: You can visit for free, although the charges will vary for each shop.

Closest City or Town: Cambridge

Physical Address:
Harvard Square
Brattle St
Cambridge, MA 02138

GPS Coordinates: 42.37344° N, 71.11899° W

Did You Know? Harvard Square has been a living space for many people since at least the seventeenth century.

Peabody Museum of Archaeology and Ethnology

The Peabody Museum on the Harvard University campus explores the history of the many cultures of the world. The museum highlights ethnological discoveries from around the Americas, objects from indigenous peoples of Asia, and art pieces from Oceania.

The museum has permanent exhibits about Hispanic cultures and the influence of the Roman Catholic faith. There are also exhibits on Latin American native cultures and how indigenous people created many objects of value.

Best Time to Visit: The museum is open throughout the year, although it is easier to access when classes are not in session.

Pass/Permit/Fees: Admission is $15 for adults and $10 for children.

Closest City or Town: Cambridge

Physical Address:
Peabody Museum of Archaeology and Ethnology
11 Divinity Ave
Cambridge, MA 02138

GPS Coordinates: 42.37830° N, 71.11491° W

Did You Know? The museum hosts thousands of maps and site plans. These guides include details on how many archeological sites were developed worldwide.

The Hahvahd Tour

Experience the unique history of Harvard University on the Hahvahd Tour, which includes the many historic buildings and features that make the university one of the most iconic in the world.

The tour will bring you to several of the famous buildings on campus, including University and Massachusetts halls: the Widener, Houghton, and Lamont libraries; and the Memorial Church.

The tour also showcases the history of the campus and its formation in 1636. You'll notice the statue of John Harvard, the Puritan minister who made a deathbed bequest of books to promote the founding of the college in Cambridge.

Best Time to Visit: Visit during the summer months when the campus isn't as busy.

Pass/Permit/Fees: Fees for tours will vary throughout the year. Expect to spend $20 to $30 per person.

Closest City or Town: Cambridge

Physical Address:
The Hahvahd Tour
1400 Massachusetts Ave
Cambridge, MA 02138

GPS Coordinates: 42.37514° N, 71.11636° W

Did You Know? The school's motto, "Veritas," is the Latin word for "truth."

Washington's Headquarters National Historic Site

George Washington used the Longfellow House in Cambridge as his headquarters from 1775 to 1776. The site is now operated by the National Park Service. The building contains many exhibits about its role as Washington's headquarters and the life of Henry Wadsworth Longfellow, the poet who lived in the home for nearly 50 years after Washington left the property. The house was built in 1759 for John Vassall, who was a loyalist. The house and all his other properties were confiscated in September 1774. Vassall fled to Boston and was later exiled to England, where he died in 1792. The building was used as a temporary hospital after the battles of Lexington and Concord in 1775.

Best Time to Visit: The house is available to tour on weekends. Appointments for a tour are strongly encouraged.

Pass/Permit/Fees: There are no fees for visiting or tours.

Closest City or Town: Cambridge

Physical Address:
Longfellow House
105 Brattle St
Cambridge, MA 02138

GPS Coordinates: 42.37692° N, 71.12629° W

Did You Know? Scaled-down replicas of the house were sold by Sears in the early twentieth century.

Monomoy National Wildlife Refuge

The refuge is an excellent spot for surf fishing spots, and visitors can also harvest soft-shell clams, razor clams, sea clams, and quahogs. Monomoy is a Western Hemisphere Shorebird Reserve Network Regional site and an Important Bird Area because of its significance to migratory shorebirds.

An exhibit room at the visitor center has information about the native wildlife of Monomoy. Binoculars are available to borrow. You can see songbirds, shorebirds, horseshoe crabs, and the occasional seal on the Morris Island trail. Breeding, wintering, foraging, and resting birds can be observed offshore.

Best Time to Visit: The refuge is open from 10 a.m. to 4 p.m. from June 1 through September 7.

Pass/Permit/Fees: There is no charge to visit the refuge, but you need a license to fish and a town permit for shell fishing.

Closest City or Town: Chatham

Physical Address:
Monomoy National Wildlife Refuge Admin Building and Visitor Contact Station
1 Wikis Way
Chatham, MA 02633

GPS Coordinates: 41.66074°N, 69.95935° W

Did You Know? The island was home to the Monomoy Island Gunnery Range from 1944 until 1951.

Chesterfield Gorge Reservation

Explore the beauty of the Chesterfield Gorge Reservation on the East Branch of the Westfield River. The gorge is about 30 feet deep, and the forest surrounding it has oak, hemlock, and pine trees. You'll also find many wild turkeys and bears throughout the park.

The stone abutments of a historic bridge are visible across the river. The bridge was built in approximately 1762 as a key link in the old post road between Albany, NY, and Boston. British soldiers marched over this bridge to Boston after they had been defeated in the Battle of Saratoga, NY, in 1777. Floodwaters swept the bridge away in 1835.

Best Time to Visit: The fall is an outstanding time because the trees will start changing color, and their foliage will be on display.

Pass/Permit/Fees: You can visit the reserve for free.

Closest City or Town: Chesterfield

Physical Address:
Chesterfield Gorge Reservation
River Rd
West Chesterfield, MA 01084

GPS Coordinates: 42.39328° N, 72.88026° W

Did You Know? You can reach the floor of the gorge during low-water periods, but this is not recommended because there are no paths to the bottom of the gorge. The reserve doesn't allow rock climbing.

Sleepy Hollow Cemetery

The Sleepy Hollow Cemetery, dedicated in 1855, is the burial site for many people who lived in Concord. The cemetery contains the final resting places of prominent authors in a section known as Author's Ridge.

Some of the famous authors who are buried at the cemetery are Ralph Waldo Emerson, Henry David Thoreau, Nathaniel Hawthorne, and Louisa May Alcott.

Best Time to Visit: The cemetery is open during daylight hours.

Pass/Permit/Fees: It is open to the public free of charge.

Closest City or Town: Concord

Physical Address:
Sleepy Hollow Cemetery
Bedford St
Concord, MA 01742

GPS Coordinates: 42.46202° N, 71.34707° W

Did You Know? Visitors often leave pens, pencils, and other writing items on the graves of the authors buried here.

Walden Pond

Walden Pond in the Middlesex County town of Concord is famous for inspiring Henry David Thoreau's famous 1854 book *Walden*. He lived for two years in a cabin on the northern end of the pond. The original cabin no longer exists, but a marker shows where it was. There is also an approximate replica of what the cabin was like.

The Pond Path will take you along the entire body of the pond. The shore is less than 2 miles long. You can also enjoy boating or fishing at various parts of the pond. The eastern part has a small beach area and a boat access site.

Best Time to Visit:
Walden Pond is easy to access during the summer season. The state reservation group limits access to about a thousand people at a time, so contact the area first for information on whether parking or access is available.

Pass/Permit/Fees: Walden Pond is free to visit.

Closest City or Town: Concord

Physical Address:
Thoreau Cabin Site
Pond Path
Concord, MA 01742

GPS Coordinates: 42.43884° N, 71.33953° W

Did You Know? Walden Pond is a kettle hole pond. It was formed about 10,000 years ago after various glaciers melted following the last ice age.

Cahoon Museum of American Art

The Cahoon Museum of American Art is in the expanded former home and studio of Ralph and Martha Cahoon. It celebrates their legacy by displaying some of their art and preserving their stately Colonial Georgian home. The house was built between 1775 and 1782. The Cahoons bought it in 1945. After Ralph's death in 1982, Martha sold the home to Rosemary Rapp, who turned it into a museum, although Martha continued to live in four rooms on the ground floor until her death in December 1999 at the age of 94.

The Cahoon features changing exhibits on a variety of American artists and their work. For information on current exhibits, visit the museum website.

Best Time to Visit: The museum is open March through December from 10 a.m. to 4 p.m. It's closed Monday and Tuesday.

Pass/Permit/Fees: Admission is $10 for adults, $8 for seniors over age 60, $8 for students, and free for children up to age 12.

Closest City or Town: Cotuit

Physical Address:
Cahoon Museum of American Art
4676 Falmouth Rd
Cotuit, MA 02635

GPS Coordinates: 41.63824° N, 70.45082° W

Did You Know? Ralph Cahoon was known for his whimsical paintings of mermaids.

Fairbanks House

The Fairbanks House in the Norfolk County town of Dedham is North America's oldest timber-frame house. It was built around 1637 and was owned by eight generations of the Fairbanks family over a 268-year period.

The house is open for tours. You can see the original workshop and observe many original pieces of furniture from the property. The building was expanded over the years, but its design has remained untouched since about 1800. The house has more than doubled in size with the addition of two full wings, a workshop, and several small expansions.

Best Time to Visit: The house is open for tours from April to October. Reservations are strongly encouraged.

Pass/Permit/Fees: Admission is $15 for adults and $8 for children.

Closest City or Town: Dedham

Physical Address:
Fairbanks House Museum c. 1637
511 East St
Dedham, MA 02026

GPS Coordinates: 42.24342° N, 71.16768° W

Did You Know? The building has been confirmed to be the continent's oldest wood house through dendrochronology, a study where tree rings are measured and dated. Some of the planks in the construction process came from trees that were felled in 1637.

Fort Hill Trail/Captain Penniman House

Fort Hill Trail is a 1-mile loop that crosses open fields, connects with the Red Maple Swamp Trail, and offers spectacular vistas of the Nauset Marsh area. Atop Fort Hill, Captain and Mrs. Edward Penniman built the Penniman House in 1868.

A 2.5-story, wood-frame structure with a mansard roof, it was styled after the French Second Empire Period (1855–1870). There are a total of nine bedrooms and a cupola above. The front stair boasts a handsome mahogany newel, handrail, and turned balusters. Flocked wallpaper and ceiling paper were hung in 1885 in the northwest parlor.

Best Time to Visit: The house is open from 6 a.m. to midnight daily but will sometimes cease tours during the winter or in the case of renovations. Summer is the best time to hike and have a chance to tour the house.

Pass/Permit/Fees: There is a free car park nearby.

Closest City or Town: Eastham

Physical Address:
Captain Penniman House
70 Fort Hill Rd
Eastham, MA 02642

GPS Coordinates: 41.8697° N, 69.9854° W

Did You Know? The National Park Service installed reproduction wallpaper in the 1980s based on original designs documented by photographs and physical remainders.

Highfield Hall and Gardens

This attraction combines a magnificent Victorian mansion with beautiful gardens near downtown Falmouth. The mansion is one of the few remaining examples of stick-style Queen Anne architecture in the Northeast, and it is surrounded by nearly 400 acres of public conservation land and walking trails.

In addition to its historical and architectural value, Highfield Hall offers a variety of art exhibits, culinary classes, family programs, musical performances, and educational opportunities.

Best Time to Visit: Estate walks are held on the first and third Sunday of the month, June through October, from noon to 1 p.m., if weather permits.

Pass/Permit/Fees: Admission is $10 for adults and free for children under age 12 or active military.

Closest City or Town: Falmouth

Physical Address:
Highfield Hall & Gardens
56 Highfield Dr
Falmouth, MA 02540

GPS Coordinates: 41.55791° N, 70.62922° W

Did You Know? Built by the Beebe family of Boston in 1878, Highfield Hall was one of the first summer mansions on Cape Cod.

Lake Cochituate

Lake Cochituate is in the middle of Cochituate State Park outside Framingham. The lake is about 625 acres in surface area. It's actually made up of three linked ponds: North Pond, Middle Pond, and South Pond.

The lake has a few public beach areas, including Wayland Beach to the east and Saxonville Beach to the northwest. These beaches offer many open piers for boating activities.

Best Time to Visit:
You will enjoy seeing the trees around the lake change colors in the fall.

Pass/Permit/Fees:
Boat rentals are available through many charters around the lake. Their charges will vary by each option.

Closest City or Town:
Framingham

Physical Address:
Wayland Town Beach
25 Parkland Dr
Wayland, MA 01778

GPS Coordinates:
42.31675° N, 71.37677° W

Did You Know?
Lake Cochituate was originally developed as a reservoir for the city of Boston. The lake no longer serves that purpose and is open to the public today.

Good Harbor Beach

The small beach space at Good Harbor Beach in Gloucester is a pleasant escape from daily life. The sand is plentiful and smooth, and the water is ideal for bodysurfing during high tide.

You can walk to nearby Salt Island during low tide. The small island is to the east and has a few additional sand spaces alongside a forested area.

Best Time to Visit: The limited space on the beach makes it hard for people to find a spot during some points in the day. Be sure to arrive early for the best opportunities.

Pass/Permit/Fees: Parking at the beach is $30 per vehicle on weekdays and $35 on weekends and holidays. The rates are lower after Labor Day, but the beach will be open during the offseason when the weather permits.

Closest City or Town: Gloucester

Physical Address:
Good Harbor Beach
99 Thatcher Rd
Gloucester, MA 01930

GPS Coordinates: 42.62061° N, 70.63254° W

Did You Know? Dogs are allowed on the beach during the offseason.

Hammond Castle Museum

Inventor John Hays Hammond Jr. (1888–1965) built this castle in the late 1920s on a bluff overlooking the Atlantic Ocean. The castle includes large stone archways, windows, wooden facades, and other architectural elements from the Old World. A connoisseur of art, Hammond added a large collection of artifacts for display. One of the most interesting items is the gigantic pipe organ containing 8,400 pipes. Guided and self-guided tours are offered. Visitors can tour the dining room, library, study, exhibit rooms, kitchen, guest bedrooms, an inner courtyard, the northern towers, and the great hall.

Best Time to Visit: The museum is open between 10 a.m. and 4 p.m. every day from May through October. It's only open Friday to Sunday during other months of the year.

Pass/Permit/Fees: Admission is $18 for adults, $15 for seniors over age 65, $10 for children ages 5–12, and free for children under age 5.

Closest City or Town: Gloucester

Physical Address:
Hammond Castle Museum
80 Hesperus Ave
Gloucester, MA 01930

GPS Coordinates: 42.58608° N, 70.69240° W

Did You Know? Hammond Castle has been the setting for several movies and TV shows, including Elizabeth Montgomery's sitcom *Bewitched*.

Monument Mountain

You can climb more than 1,600 feet to the top of Monument Mountain in Great Barrington in Berkshire County. Monument Mountain is a quartzite mountain that offers a view of the Berkshires and the Catskills in New York. The Devil's Pulpit formation is one of the most familiar features. It's a stone pillar on the southwest side that stands on its own without support. The northeast area also has a small waterfall.

Best Time to Visit: The summer season is the easiest time to visit because most of the trails that lead to the peak of the mountain are open and safe to travel then.

Pass/Permit/Fees: It costs $6 to park at the mountain site. Hunting is permitted during the proper seasons, but it requires a hunting permit or license.

Closest City or Town: Great Barrington

Physical Address:
Monument Mountain Parking Space
546 Stockbridge Rd
Great Barrington, MA 01230

GPS Coordinates: 42.25776° N, 73.34635° W

Did You Know? Nathaniel Hawthorne and Herman Melville enjoyed a picnic hike up Monument Mountain on August 5, 1850. When a thunderstorm forced them to seek refuge in a cave, their long discussion inspired ideas for a novel that Melville was working on titled *Moby-Dick*, which he dedicated to Hawthorne.

Beauport, the Sleeper-McCann House

Beauport, which sits on a rock ledge overlooking Gloucester Harbor, was the 56-room summer home of one of America's first professional interior designers, Henry Davis Sleeper. He filled the house with his large collection of architectural artifacts, fine art, folk art, and other collectible materials. Charles and Helena Woolworth McCann bought the house after Sleeper's death in 1934 and made very few changes, but they did add their own extensive collection of porcelain.

The McCann heirs in 1947 donated the property to the Society for the Protection of New England Antiquities, which is now Historic New England, and that organization currently operates the property as a house museum.

Best Time to Visit: The house is open May 27 through October 16 from 10 a.m. to 3 p.m. except for Monday, Tuesday, and Wednesday. Tours are every half an hour.

Pass/Permit/Fees: Admission is $20 for adults, $17 for seniors, and $8 for children and students.

Closest City or Town: Gloucester

Physical Address:
Beauport, Sleeper-McCann House
75 Eastern Point Blvd
Gloucester, MA 01930

GPS Coordinates: 42.591111° N, 70.660556° W

Did You Know? Beauport was declared a National Historic Landmark in 2003.

Historic Deerfield

You can explore some of the oldest homes in New England in Historic Deerfield in Franklin County. The village has 11 homes built during the eighteenth century, with some dating to the 1730s. Many of the homes are open for tours. They have been refurbished to look as they did when they were first built.

Historic Deerfield offers demonstrations of textile and furniture manufacturing. It also has a collection of outfits and items used by many people in the eighteenth century. The village of Old Deerfield has been designated a National Historic Landmark District, and it's listed on the National Register of Historic Places.

Best Time to Visit: Historic Deerfield is open from June to November every year.

Pass/Permit/Fees: Admission is $15 for adults. Children under age 18 are free.

Closest City or Town: Greenfield

Physical Address:
Historic Deerfield
80 Old Main St
Deerfield, MA 01342

GPS Coordinates: 42.54713° N, 72.60408° W

Did You Know? The town of Deerfield was settled in 1673 and incorporated a few years later.

The Glacial Potholes of Shelburne Falls

Shelburne Falls is in the Deerfield River in the town of the same name. The waterfalls, which are south of the Bridge Street bridge in the center of the city, are noteworthy for their many glacial potholes. This is one of the largest collections of natural potholes in the world and the site of the largest pothole on record.

The potholes were formed near the end of the last Glacial Age. The whirlpool effect on granite stones gave these potholes a remarkably symmetrical, round shape. They are still being formed by the end-of-winter snow melt. The water flowing through has eroded through the hard gneiss surface. The process helped give the rocks a unique appearance.

Best Time to Visit: It's easier to see these potholes during the spring and summer because the water won't be frozen.

Pass/Permit/Fees: The waterfall is free to visit.

Closest City or Town: Greenfield

Physical Address:
Shelburne Falls Potholes
J726+W7
Shelburne Falls, MA 01370

GPS Coordinates: 42.60291° N, 72.73968° W

Did You Know? The town of Shelburne Falls has a visitor's center open from May to October. You can learn more about the waterfall and other features of the town from the center.

Crane Beach on the Crane Estate

The Crane Estate in Ipswich is a 2,100-acre area that includes Castle Hill, a Tudor Revival mansion near the shore of Ipswich Bay. The estate includes a private rose garden, 21 outbuildings, and landscapes surrounded by sea and salt marshes.

Crane Beach is the most popular part of the estate for visitors. It has about 5 miles of hiking trails that go through many sand dunes and forested areas. The beach is open for swimming during the summer season.

Best Time to Visit: Most beach activities take place during the summer, including weekly outdoor picnic concerts.

Pass/Permit/Fees: It is free for Ipswich residents to visit after buying an annual beach-parking sticker. Nonresidents must pay a charge, which varies depending on the day of the week and the time of the year. The mansion is accessible at $10 per car.

Closest City or Town: Ipswich

Physical Address:
Castle Hill on the Crane Estate (continue down Argilla Rd to reach the Crane Beach trail at Castle Neck)
290 Argilla Rd
Ipswich, MA 01938

GPS Coordinates: 42.68499° N, 70.76720° W

Did You Know? The piping plover can be found in many parts of the beach and estate area. The bird is considered a threatened species.

The Mount, Edith Wharton's Home

The author Edith Wharton (1862–1937) wrote classic novels such as *The Age of Innocence* and *The House of Mirth*, as well as works on architecture, design, and travel. She designed and built this estate in 1902, and she and her husband, Edward, lived here until 1911.

The current estate contains 49.5 acres. An Italian walled garden, formal flower garden, alpine rock garden, lime walk, and extensive grass terraces have been restored. In addition to the main house, the Lord and Burnham greenhouse and the Georgian Revival gatehouse and stable have also been carefully restored.

Best Time to Visit: Between May and October, the home is open daily from 10 a.m. to 5 p.m. From November through February, it's only open Saturday and Sunday.

Pass/Permit/Fees: Admission is $20 for adults, $18 for seniors over age 65, $13 for students with ID, and free for children under 18.

Closest City or Town: Lenox

Physical Address:
The Mount, Edith Wharton's Home
2 Plunkett St
Lenox, MA 01240

GPS Coordinates: 42.335579° N, 73.2829° W

Did You Know? Edith Wharton published more than 40 books in 40 years.

Minute Man National Historical Park

Minute Man National Historical Park is home to the Lexington Green, a town common where the first shots of the American Revolutionary War were fired on April 19, 1775. The park contains many buildings preserved from the eighteenth century, including the Hartwell Tavern (1733) and a few farm properties.

You can walk down the trail to see where Paul Revere was captured following his midnight ride, *The Minute Man* statue, and the Captain William Smith House, which dates to 1692. The site also includes an obelisk believed to be the country's oldest memorial to its war dead.

Best Time to Visit: The park is open throughout the year.

Pass/Permit/Fees: The park is free to visit.

Closest City or Town: Lexington

Physical Address:
Minute Man National Historical Park
250 N Great Rd
Lincoln, MA 01773

GPS Coordinates: 42.44869° N, 71.26794° W

Did You Know? The Lexington Green is one of a handful of sites in the United States where the American flag is required by law to fly 24 hours a day.

Coolidge Reservation

The Coolidge Reservation in Manchester-by-the-Sea is a 66-acre nature reserve on land once owned by Thomas Jefferson Coolidge. It offers amazing views of the Massachusetts Bay and the North Shore as well as an unusual variety of natural settings. The grassy field of the Ocean Lawn on the tip of the reserve is the former site of the Coolidge family's Georgian mansion. Bungalow Hill, the reservation's highest point, offers a panoramic view of the sea. The woodland is home to a wide array of birds and other wildlife. Clarke Pond provides a habitat for ducks and geese as well as feeding grounds for herons and shorebirds. The pond is surrounded by wetlands that feature cattail, bulrush, and cordgrass, along with colorful trout lilies, jack-in-the-pulpit, and swamp buttercups.

Best Time to Visit: The Ocean Lawn is open on weekends. The rest of the property is open throughout the week.

Pass/Permit/Fees: There is no admission charge, but the Trustees of Reservations do encourage donations.

Closest City or Town: Manchester-by-the-Sea

Physical Address:
Coolidge Reservation
15 Coolidge Point
Manchester-by-the-Sea, MA 01944

GPS Coordinates: 42.57414° N, 70.72903° W

Did You Know? The Boston skyline can be seen from the reserve on a clear day. The city is about 30 miles from the reserve.

Singing Beach

Singing Beach in Manchester-by-the-Sea is unique for having a sand body that makes a singing-like sound when it's dry. The textures of the sand particles cause them to make noises when the wind blows.

Singing Beach is about half a mile wide and features a bathhouse built in the 1920s. The beach has a recreational area for ball sports.

Best Time to Visit: The bathhouse is open from Memorial Day to Labor Day. Dogs are permitted on the beach from October to April.

Pass/Permit/Fees: Parking is $25 for nonresidents.

Closest City or Town: Manchester-by-the-Sea

Physical Address:
Singing Beach
119 Beach St
Manchester-by-the-Sea, MA 01944

GPS Coordinates: 42.56955° N, 70.76026° W

Did You Know? The beach features views of rock formations around the Manchester-by-the-Sea area.

Mashpee Wampanoag Museum

The museum is located in the Bourne-Avant House, which was built about 1793 by the great-grandson of Richard Bourne, a missionary. Although the interior has been adapted for use as a museum, many original features were retained, among them a Greek Revival fireplace mantel in the parlor. A Wampanoag named Timothy Pocknet bought the house in 1863. Mabel Avant, a Wampanoag elder, and tribal historian, had owned it for many years. The Wampanoag Tribe opened the house as a museum in 1973, but legal conflicts over land shut it down. It was finally returned to the tribe in 1998 and has reopened as a museum. Displays include ancient artifacts and other Native American heirlooms, including tools, baskets, hunting and fishing equipment, weapons, and domestic utensils.

Best Time to Visit: The museum is open Monday, Wednesday, and Friday from 10 a.m. to 4 p.m.

Pass/Permit/Fees: Admission is $8 for adults, $5 for children ages 6–18, and $7 for seniors.

Closest City or Town: Mashpee

Physical Address:
Mashpee Wampanoag Indian Msm
414 Main St
Mashpee, MA 02649

GPS Coordinates: 41.649167° N, 70.486667° W

Did You Know? Eighty-five percent of the Wampanoag people live within 20 miles of the museum.

Cisco Beach

Cisco Beach, located in the southwestern part of Nantucket, is one of the most popular beaches on the island. It's a popular site for surfing because some of the best waves in Nantucket can be found here. The beautiful white sand has not been heavily disturbed by visitors. The area is also open for swimming. Lifeguards are on duty during the summer.

Surfboards and boogie boards are available for rent. There's a food truck at the beach on most good days, and port-a-johns are also available.

Best Time to Visit: Conditions are their safest during the summer. It's advisable to get to the beach by 11:30 a.m. because parking is limited.

Pass/Permit/Fees: There are no admission charges for Cisco Beach.

Closest City or Town: Nantucket

Physical Address:
Cisco Beach
1 Dirt Rd
Nantucket, MA 02554

GPS Coordinates: 41.25249° N, 70.15779° W

Did You Know? Multiple surfing schools throughout Nantucket can help you learn how to surf and enjoy the waves on Cisco Beach.

Nantucket

Nantucket is a popular island about 30 miles south of Cape Cod. Like nearby Martha's Vineyard, it is a summer colony that grows in population during the summer. The central town of Nantucket is home to many boutiques, restaurants, and fishing piers. The cobblestone-lined streets produce a quaint look. You will find many beaches throughout Nantucket, including Cisco and Madaket beaches. The Great Point Lighthouse appears on the far northern end of the island, while the Brant Point Lighthouse is closer to the main town.

Best Time to Visit: Most of the attractions around Nantucket are only open during the summer months.

Pass/Permit/Fees: The cost to take a ferry ranges from $20 to $40 for a round trip. The total will vary depending on which line you choose. You can also bring a vehicle to Nantucket, but it will cost $200 or more to reserve space on a ferry.

Closest City or Town: Nantucket

Physical Address:
Nantucket Information Bureau
25 Federal St
Nantucket, MA 02554

GPS Coordinates: 41.27881° N, 70.07941° W

Did You Know? The permanent population on Nantucket is around 15,000 people, but it increases to about 50,000 during the summer.

Martha's Vineyard

Martha's Vineyard is a popular island and summer colony south of Cape Cod. The island houses many resorts and bed-and-breakfast sites. There are many excellent dining spaces around the island as well. You'll find a variety of opportunities for birding, hiking, boating, and skating throughout Martha's Vineyard. Many of the beaches are on the southern end of the island, with Long Point Beach and Squibnocket Beach being among the most popular. The Cape Poge Lighthouse is to the east on Chappaquiddick Island, while the Gay Head Light is to the west in Aquinnah.

Best Time to Visit: The summer months are the most active. About 17,000 people live on the island year-round, but the population rises to 100,000 in the summer.

Pass/Permit/Fees: You have to take a ferry to reach the island. An average ferry ride is $20 to $30 for adults for a round trip, and prices for children are about half that amount. It costs more to bring a vehicle onto the ferry.

Closest City or Town: New Bedford

Physical Address:
Martha's Vineyard
Pond Rd
West Tisbury, MA 02575

GPS Coordinates: 41.39955° N, 70.61636° W

Did You Know? Hereditary deafness is common among many natives on the island. The deaf community is substantial.

New Bedford Art Museum

You will see many exciting works of art at the New Bedford Art Museum. This museum near the Whaling Historical Park in New Bedford has galleries showcasing art from around the world.

The museum also hosts exhibitions displaying local artwork and unique trends in the art world. The place also periodically appoints an artist in residence, usually from the local area. The Creative Courts program is popular because it entails creating unique art designs on basketball courts in the region.

Best Time to Visit: The museum has many exhibits featuring different themes and artists, so visit the museum's website to learn more about what is currently on display.

Pass/Permit/Fees: Admission is $8 for adults and $5 for children.

Closest City or Town: New Bedford

Physical Address:
New Medford Art Museum
608 Pleasant St
New Bedford, MA 02740

GPS Coordinates: 41.63530° N, 70.92607° W

Did You Know? The museum also offers art programs for adults and children. These include classes where people can learn about art concepts and create their own pieces.

New Bedford Seaport Cultural District

The charm of the New Bedford Seaport Cultural District comes from its vast culture. This district near the waterfront features 49 cultural attractions and 29 creative economy businesses. The New Bedford Art Museum, New Bedford Ballet, and New Bedford Symphony Orchestra are all based in the seaport district. The Whaling National Historic Park is also in the area, which is lined with many cobblestone streets. You'll have a vast array of restaurants to choose from in the district, including an extensive number of seafood spots. You can also shop for antiques, boutique items, and gifts here.

Best Time to Visit: You'll find a full array of events here throughout the year. The Oktoberfest events in October and the Holiday Happenings programs in December are among the most popular. The New Bedford Jazz Fest also occurs here in June.

Pass/Permit/Fees: Prices will vary by venue and activity.

Closest City or Town: New Bedford

Physical Address:
New Bedford Whaling National Historical Park
38 Bethel St
New Bedford, MA 02740

GPS Coordinates: 41.63611° N, 70.92330° W

Did You Know? New Bedford was founded in 1787, making it slightly younger than some of the other cities around the commonwealth.

New Bedford Whaling Museum

Explore the history of whaling at the New Bedford Whaling Museum. The venue has a vast collection of whaling items, including thousands of pieces of scrimshaw engravings prepared by whalers. There are five whale skeletons on display here, along with many weapons and other items used by whalers.

The *Lagoda* is a half-scale whaling ship model available for tours at the museum. The ship illustrates the habitats in which whalers lived when sailing and working on the sea. The museum also looks at modern marine life and explores the value of whales and many other mammals. Part of the museum showcases seals that are present throughout much of New England's coastline.

Best Time to Visit: The museum is open throughout the year.

Pass/Permit/Fees: Admission is $19 for adults and $9 for children.

Closest City or Town: New Bedford

Physical Address:
New Bedford Whaling Museum
18 Johnny Cake Hill
New Bedford, MA 02740

GPS Coordinates: 41.63559° N, 70.92322° W

Did You Know? Whaling has been practiced in many forms since at least the ninth century.

Parker River National Wildlife Refuge

You will find some exciting natural sights around Parker River National Wildlife Refuge in Newburyport. The refuge contains nearly 5,000 acres of land. There are beach spaces around the refuge and many inland bodies of water throughout the region.

The Great Marsh houses freshwater and saltwater grasses. The refuge helps support nearly 300 species of animals who call the area home. The piping plover and saltmarsh sparrow are two endangered species that are studied at the refuge. The plover is notable for its black neck pattern.

Best Time to Visit: Visit during one of the migratory times of the year because many birds will arrive in the refuge as they travel north or south for the season.

Pass/Permit/Fees: It costs $5 for cars to enter and $2 for bicycles and pedestrians.

Closest City or Town: Newburyport

Physical Address:
Parker River National Wildlife Refuge
Refuge Rd
Newbury, MA 01951

GPS Coordinates: 42.79171° N, 70.80986° W

Did You Know? The Atlantic Flyway goes through the refuge site. The flyway is a migratory path for birds that starts in Greenland and moves down the Atlantic Coast toward the tropical parts of South America.

Quabbin Overlook

You will find beautiful views of the Quabbin Reservoir and many parts of north-central Massachusetts from the Quabbin Overlook near New Salem. The reservoir is to the south of the overlook.

The Quabbin Overlook is home to many birds, including the scarlet tanager, hermit thrush, and least flycatcher. Bald eagles can also be seen in the area.

The Quabbin Visitor Center offers exhibits, brochures, books, and videos about the reservoir's management and history.

Best Time to Visit: The overlook is popular in the fall because the trees are changing colors, and various birds can be seen migrating.

Pass/Permit/Fees: Visiting the overlook is free.

Closest City or Town: New Salem

Physical Address:
Quabbin Overlook
26 S Main St #32
New Salem, MA 01355

GPS Coordinates: 42.49945° N, 72.33096° W

Did You Know? The Quabbin Reservoir was created in the 1930s as a water supply for Boston. The residents of four towns were relocated to make room for over 400 billion gallons of water. After its completion in 1939, it took seven years for rainwater to fill the reservoir.

Mass MoCA

Sprague Electric occupied this complex of buildings until 1985, and a year later, a group from the Williams College Museum of Art selected it as a space where they could exhibit large works of modern and contemporary art. Years of fundraising brought in $8 million in private money and an $18.6 million state grant that led to the creation of Mass MoCA, which opened in 1999. The museum has become one of the country's largest centers for contemporary visual art and performing arts. It originally contained 19 galleries and 100,000 square feet, and two major expansions have increased that to 250,000 square feet. Mass MoCA also presents more than 75 performances of a wide range of music.

Best Time to Visit: The museum is open Wednesday through Monday from 10 a.m. to 5 p.m.

Pass/Permit/Fees: Admission is $20 for adults, $18 for seniors and veterans, $12 for students with ID, and $8 for children ages 6–16. Children under age 6 are free.

Closest City or Town: North Adams

Physical Address:
MASS MoCA
1040 Mass MoCA Way
North Adams, MA 01247

GPS Coordinates: 42.701389° N, 73.116389° W

Did You Know? The official name is Massachusetts Museum of Contemporary Art, but everyone simply calls it "Mass MoCA."

Beer Can Museum

Beer cans have been produced since the 1930s and have evolved in many ways since. The Beer Can Museum shows these changes over time. The museum is inside Ye Ol' Watering Hole, a bar in southern Northampton.

The museum has more than 5,000 beer cans, several of which date back to the 1930s. Many of these cans come from imported beers, and some of them date to before cans were made of aluminum. Some feature tab tops that were used before the pop-top became the industry standard.

Best Time to Visit: The museum is open during the bar's regular operating hours.

Pass/Permit/Fees: You can visit for free, but you must be at least 21 years of age to enter.

Closest City or Town: Northampton

Physical Address:
Beer Can Museum
287 Pleasant St
Northampton, MA 01060

GPS Coordinates: 42.31677° N, 72.62610° W

Did You Know? The most popular beer cans in the collection are the two cans of Billy Beer from 1976. The beer was produced by the brother of President Jimmy Carter.

Hancock Shaker Village

This 750-acre living history museum is also the oldest working farm in the Berkshires. The Round Stone Barn is an amazing example of engineering and architecture, and the farm also features heritage-breed animals and extensive gardens. The museum collection includes thousands of Shaker artifacts and furniture on display in 20 authentic historic buildings.

Several special events are held in the course of the year, including Baby Animals on the Shaker Farm in the spring and Country Fair in the fall. For a complete schedule of events, visit the Village's website.

Best Time to Visit: The village is open from April through November.

Pass/Permit/Fees: Admission is $20 for adults, $8 for children ages 13–17, and free for children ages 12 and under.

Closest City or Town: Pittsfield

Physical Address:
Hancock Shaker Village
1843 W Housatonic St
Pittsfield, MA 01201

GPS Coordinates: 42.430283° N, 73.343289° W

Did You Know? Hancock Shaker Village was added to the National Register of Historic Places and declared a National Historic Landmark District in 1968.

Lake Onota

Lake Onota in Pittsfield features about 600 acres of land divided into two basins. The lake is a popular site for boating, with launches on the southern and eastern parts of the lake. It is also a noteworthy site for fishing and swimming.

The lake has a small beach area to the east. Some rowing clubs have events here as well. Nearby Williams College offers rowing activities, including competitions for the school's varsity men's and women's rowing programs.

Best Time to Visit: The lake hosts concerts during the summer season.

Pass/Permit/Fees: While you can get on the water for free, you will need a permit for fishing.

Closest City or Town: Pittsfield

Physical Address:
Onota Lake
Lakeway Dr
Pittsfield, MA 01201

GPS Coordinates: 42.46853° N, 73.28069° W

Did You Know? Many of the properties on the lakefront were built in the late nineteenth century. They were used mainly as summer homes for the wealthy.

Mount Greylock

Experience Massachusetts from up high on Mount Greylock. At 3,489 feet, it is the highest point in the commonwealth. The mountain is in Berkshire County in the northwestern part of the state. Mount Greylock also provides views of New York and Vermont and parts of New Hampshire on a clear day.

The surrounding park has about 70 miles of hiking and climbing trails. The Appalachian Train goes through the area as well. The area surrounding the mountain also houses the Veterans War Memorial Tower. The tower is about 93 feet high and has an Art Deco-inspired design.

Best Time to Visit: The mountain is popular for skiing and snowboarding in the winter, but most of the area is easier to access in the summer since many roads are closed from November through June.

Pass/Permit/Fees: Parking is $10 for non-residents or $5 for residents.

Closest City or Town: Pittsfield

Physical Address:
Mount Greylock State Reservation
30 Rockwell Rd
Lanesborough, MA 01237

GPS Coordinates: 42.63731° N, 73.16691° W

Did You Know? The reservation here was formed in 1898 and was the first area in the commonwealth dedicated to forest protection.

Pontoosuc Lake

Pontoosuc Lake, located north of Pittsfield, is a popular site for boating and other water activities. The lake has a few launching spots for boats. It is open for fishing, with perch, trout, sunfish, and pike among the most popular fish to catch here.

The area is popular for snowmobiling in the winter, but people will find it ideal for biking and waterskiing during the summer. The quaint forest surroundings make it one of the most popular places for people to visit while in Massachusetts.

Best Time to Visit: The lake is busiest on summer weekends.

Pass/Permit/Fees: You can access the lake for free, but you'll require a permit for fishing.

Closest City or Town: Pittsfield

Physical Address:
Pontoosuc Lake Parking
North St
Pittsfield, MA 01201

GPS Coordinates: 42.49465° N, 73.24789° W

Did You Know? Most of the lake is shallow, with an average depth of about 14 feet. However, parts of the lake are up to 30 feet deep, so caution is encouraged.

Tanglewood

Tanglewood is a musical venue in Lenox on the far western end of the state in Berkshire County. It opened in 1938, with the Koussevitzky Music Shed offering about 5,000 seats of space at a fan-shaped property.

Tanglewood hosts many classical music concerts throughout the year. It also holds some jazz and contemporary music events, including the annual Tanglewood Music Festival every summer. The venue is the summer home for the Boston Symphony Orchestra.

Best Time to Visit: The schedule of shows varies from year to year. Visit Tanglewood's website for details on what shows are coming. Most of the events here are in the summer.

Pass/Permit/Fees: Ticket prices will vary by event.

Closest City or Town: Pittsfield

Physical Address:
Tanglewood
297 West St
Lenox, MA 01240

GPS Coordinates: 42.35284° N, 73.31070° W

Did You Know? Tanglewood has a secondary indoor venue called Seiji Ozawa Hall, which can accommodate 1,200 people.

Mayflower II and Plimoth Plantation

The *Mayflower* that brought Pilgrims to the New World in 1620 is represented by a replica, *Mayflower II*. The ship is open for tours, so you can see where the Pilgrims lived for months while sailing to Massachusetts.

The *Mayflower II* is not far from Plimoth Plantation, a living history museum that recreates the original Plymouth Colony. The museum has many recreated houses and other buildings where the Pilgrims lived after arriving.

Best Time to Visit: The ship and plantation are both open to visitors throughout the year.

Pass/Permit/Fees: Tickets to the *Mayflower II* are $15 for adults and $12 for children. You can visit the entire complex with a Heritage Pass, which is $42.50 for adults and $27.50 for children.

Closest City or Town: Plymouth

Physical Address:
Plimoth Plantation Parking
137 Warren Ave
Plymouth, MA 02360

GPS Coordinates: 41.95946° N, 70.66275° W

Did You Know? Details on what happened with the original *Mayflower* ship remain unclear. Some parties claim to have original pieces of the *Mayflower*, but there is no way they can be verified.

Myles Standish Burial Ground

The Myles Standish Burial Ground in Duxbury was established around 1638, and it's the oldest continuously run cemetery in the country. It has about 130 graves, many of which belong to Pilgrims who arrived in the area on the *Mayflower* in 1620. The site is named for the most famous person buried here, Captain Myles Standish, who was the Plymouth Colony's chief military advisor. The cemetery was built on the site where Duxbury's first meeting house stood. Most of the stones here date to after 1750, with the ones from earlier being used mainly for people who came over on the *Mayflower*. Some of the Pilgrims buried here include George Soule, John Alden, and Priscilla Alden.

Best Time to Visit: The cemetery is open during daylight hours.

Pass/Permit/Fees: The site is open to the public.

Closest City or Town: Plymouth

Physical Address:
Myles Standish Burial Ground
Chestnut St
Duxbury, MA 02332

GPS Coordinates: 42.02532° N, 70.68754° W

Did You Know? Myles Standish was initially buried here after his death in 1656, but his body has been exhumed three separate times. Concerns about neglect of the cemetery and confusion over where his body was led to those exhumations. He was buried here one last time in 1931.

Bearskin Neck

Rockport has been a major art colony for a long time, and Bearskin Neck is the major emblem of that artistic activity. Among the great artists who worked in Rockport at various times were Winslow Homer, Edward Hopper, and John Twachtman. Bearskin Neck's famous red fishing shack, nicknamed "Motif #1," is believed to be the most painted and photographed building in the world.

More than 30 art galleries containing the work of over 400 artists are located in Rockport, many of them on Bearskin Neck. Its shops offer something for just about everyone, from souvenirs to works of art, and Bearskin Neck restaurants can satisfy every appetite, whether you want hot dogs, fried clams, or a full sit-down meal.

Best Time to Visit: Summer is when all the shops, galleries, and restaurants are open.

Pass/Permit/Fees: There is no charge to visit.

Closest City or Town: Rockport

Physical Address:
Bearskin Neck (coastal main street)
Rockport, MA 01966

GPS Coordinates: 42.66017° N, 70.61551° W

Did You Know? One story about how Bearskin Neck got its name is that a fisherman killed a bear with his fishing knife, then skinned it and draped the skin over the rocks to dry.

Halibut Point State Park

Halibut Point State Park in Rockport sits on granite deposits that are at least 400 million years old. The abandoned granite quarry is filled with water up to 60 feet deep. You'll find wildflowers of all sorts growing throughout the area. On clear days, visitors can see Mount Agamenticus 40 miles away in Maine and the Isles of Shoals off the New Hampshire coast. The park has trails and tide pools to explore, and visitors can picnic on rocky ledges. You'll also see some naturally produced granite formations, including Stone Table with Round Hole on the northern end of the park.

Best Time to Visit: You'll find many birds feeding off of the shoreline during the winter season. Loon, duck, and grebe are among the birds you will find here.

Pass/Permit/Fees: You can visit the park for free.

Closest City or Town: Rockport

Physical Address:
Halibut Point State Park Parking Lot
4 Gott Ave
Rockport, Ave MA 01966

GPS Coordinates: 42.69029° N, 70.63140° W

Did You Know? The park was used as a granite-mining space for much of the nineteenth century. The quarry was abandoned in the 1920s following the collapse of the industry, but it was repurposed as a nature reserve a few years later.

Rockport Paper House

In 1922, Elis F. Stenman, a mechanical engineer, began building a summer home in Rockport. He constructed a frame of wood with a wooden roof and floor, and he planned to use rolled-up newspaper, glued and varnished, to become insulation. But then he decided to see how well paper would hold up as a building material, and he wrapped the entire house with more than 100,000 rolled-up newspapers, most of them donated by friends and neighbors.

The house features walls, furniture, and many other items made from newspapers. There's even a piano, but it's an ordinary wooden piano wrapped in paper.

Best Time to Visit: The house is open from spring to fall.

Pass/Permit/Fees: Admission is $2 for adults and $1 for children.

Closest City or Town: Rockport

Physical Address:
Paper House
52 Pigeon Hill St
Rockport, MA 01966

GPS Coordinates: 42.67291° N, 70.63460° W

Did You Know? The newspapers used in the construction were coated with varnish to stiffen and protect them. You can read what was on the newspapers in spots where the varnish has worn.

Bewitched Statue

The town of Salem is home to a statue featuring one of the most famous fictional witches in pop culture history. The *Bewitched* statue in the center of the town portrays actress Elizabeth Montgomery, who played the famous witch Samantha on the television series of the same name. The statue shows Montgomery as Samantha sitting on a broom and flying with a crescent moon in the backdrop.

The statue was sponsored by TV Land, a television channel that focuses on classic television programs. The network has also produced statues for shows like *The Honeymooners, The Andy Griffith Show*, and *The Mary Tyler Moore Show*.

Best Time to Visit: The statue is often decorated for holidays.

Pass/Permit/Fees: The statue is accessible throughout the day. There's enough room on the broom for people to take photos posing next to the statue.

Closest City or Town: Salem

Physical Address:
Lappin Park
237-245 Essex St
Salem, MA 01970

GPS Coordinates: 42.52137° N, 70.89585° W

Did You Know? A few episodes of *Bewitched* were shot in Salem in the 1970s. They were taped there after a fire in California forced the production crew to relocate.

House of the Seven Gables

The House of the Seven Gables was built in 1668. It's distinguishable for its seven gables, which are triangular segments near the roof pitches on the building. The home was the main inspiration for Nathaniel Hawthorne's novel *The House of the Seven Gables.*

The house has been a museum since the early twentieth century. It has seventeen rooms and a massive cellar. Its wooden panels are consistent with Georgian and Colonial structures of the time. Many of the rooms have been restored with copies of various furniture items used in the home when it opened.

Best Time to Visit: The house is open year-round.

Pass/Permit/Fees: Admission is $11.

Closest City or Town: Salem

Physical Address:
The House of the Seven Gables
115 Derby St
Salem, MA 01970

GPS Coordinates: 42.52188° N, 70.88334° W

Did You Know? Some of the gables were removed for renovations in the nineteenth century. The property was restored in the twentieth century when it opened as a museum. All seven gables remain intact today.

Salem Witch Museum

The Salem Witch Museum, located near Salem Common, is dedicated to the 1692 Salem witch trials. The museum is housed in an old church building and includes 13 life-size sets displaying the history of the witch trials. The exhibits illustrate how the trials led to the deaths of many people by hanging after they were accused of practicing witchcraft.

The museum also has exhibits on the concept of witchcraft and the perceptions people have about those who are considered to be witches. It looks at witch trials in Europe from around the same time and shows how prevalent witch-hunting was in the sixteenth and seventeenth centuries.

Best Time to Visit: The museum is very popular during the Halloween season in October.

Pass/Permit/Fees: Admission is $15 for adults and $12 for children.

Closest City or Town: Salem

Physical Address:
Salem Witch Museum
19 ½ N Washington Square
Salem, MA 01970

GPS Coordinates: 42.52364° N, 70.89097° W

Did You Know? While most of the people executed during the trials were hanged, one person was crushed to death for refusing to enter a plea. The crushing entailed pressing hundreds of pounds of rocks on the person's body.

Witch House of Salem

The Witch House of Salem was built in the early seventeenth century. The house is famous for being the largest remaining building in Salem that has direct ties to the witch trials of 1692.

The wooden building includes many artifacts and documents relating to the witch trials, including a look at the court proceedings surrounding these events and how those hearings occurred.

You can also see how the property was built, and it features many architectural accents found throughout the seventeenth century. However, there is uncertainty about when the property was built.

Best Time to Visit: The venue is very popular in October.

Pass/Permit/Fees: Admission is $9.

Closest City or Town: Salem

Physical Address:
The Witch House at Salem
310 Essex St
Salem, MA 01970

GPS Coordinates: 42.52158° N, 70.89886° W

Did You Know? The home was purchased in 1675 by Jonathan Corwin, a local judge who presided over many of the hearings during the witch trials.

Heritage Museum and Gardens

The museum has a collection of more than 18,000 items, highlighted by 41 antique and classic automobiles. It also features collections of American folk art, Currier & Ives lithographs, Elmer Crowell bird carvings, and a 1908 working carousel. Made by Charles Looff, the hand-carved carousel is one of the most popular attractions at Heritage Museums & Gardens. The gardens feature several special sections, including the McInnes Garden and its Bee Sculpture, the Cape Cod Hydrangea Display Garden, the Dexter Rhododendron Garden, the McGraw Garden of the Senses, the Donald Marvin Daylily Garden, and the North American Hydrangea Test Garden.

Best Time to Visit: The gardens are most bountiful from spring through summer.

Pass/Permit/Fees: Prices vary with season and exhibits. Online advance purchase is required at the museum and gardens website.

Closest City or Town: Sandwich

Physical Address:
Heritage Museums & Gardens
67 Grove St
Sandwich, MA 02563

GPS Coordinates: 41.74944° N, 70.50769° W

Did You Know? The automobiles on display range from an 1899 Winton to a 1965 Ford Country Squire station wagon.

Museum of Bad Art

The Museum of Bad Art is an intriguing venue in Somerville that hosts unusual art pieces that the museum says are "too bad to be ignored." The art pieces include works that are noted for having unusual color patterns, poor perception, and difficult angles. But they are heralded for showcasing the passion and genuine interest the artists have for their work.

Many of the art pieces here are interesting because of how bizarre they are. Among them is a painting of a dog wearing a hula skirt while juggling some bones. There's also a George Seurat parody at the museum that features a man sitting on a toilet.

Best Time to Visit: The museum is open throughout the year.

Pass/Permit/Fees: Admission to the museum is free.

Closest City or Town: Somerville

Physical Address:
The Museum of Bad Art
55 Davis Square
Somerville, MA 02144

GPS Coordinates: 42.39689° N, 71.12266° W

Did You Know? The main principle of the museum is that the bad art should have a serious intention, but it must also have substantial flaws in its work. However, the product cannot be boring, so there should be something interesting about it.

Museum of Modern Renaissance

Somerville is home to the Museum of Modern Renaissance, a building that features many art pieces. The building was originally home to the Independent Order of Odd Fellows and then the Ancient Free and Accepted Masons. In 2002, Russian-born artists Nicholas Shaplyko and Ekaterina Sorokina bought the building and transformed it into their shared artistic vision.

The artists worked on the art throughout the entire building. They prepared fresco-style paintings with many Russian mythological figures and saturated oil colors as accents. The designs create a stained glass-like look in the building that makes it very memorable and intriguing.

Best Time to Visit: The museum is open throughout the year.

Pass/Permit/Fees: The house is free to visit, but donations are encouraged.

Closest City or Town: Somerville

Physical Address:
Museum of Modern Renaissance
115 College Ave
Somerville, MA 02144

GPS Coordinates: 42.39983° N, 71.11779° W

Did You Know? The museum's building is where the Self-Realization Fellowship, a spiritual movement, was first introduced to the United States by Paramahansa Yogananda.

Prospect Hill Monument

Prospect Hill Park in Somerville is home to a large stone tower. The monument is four stories high and features an elaborate stone body with a castle-inspired look. Its official name is Prospect Hill Memorial Flag Tower and Observatory.

Parts of the tower are open to the public. You can see much of Boston, Cambridge, and Somerville from there. Prospect Hill is where American armies were fortified during the Revolutionary War.

Best Time to Visit: The sunrise and sunset hours are great times to visit the tower because the surrounding landscape looks more dramatic and dynamic at these points.

Pass/Permit/Fees: You can visit the tower for free.

Closest City or Town: Somerville

Physical Address:
Prospect Hill Monument
68 Munroe St
Somerville, MA 02143

GPS Coordinates: 42.38169° N, 71.09353° W

Did You Know? The Grand Union Flag flies atop the tower. It is believed that when George Washington lifted the flag over the land where the tower stands, it was the first time that any American flag was raised.

The Mμseum

The Mμseum, or the Tiny Museum as it is also called, is considered the world's smallest museum. Only 8 inches deep and 16 inches long, it is built on the side of a building in Somerville next to a sandwich shop.

The Mμseum hosts various miniatures created by artists from the area. These items are often inspired by local events. Somerville claims to have more artists per capita than any other town or city in the United States.

Best Time to Visit: The Mμseum's selection of items changes during the year.

Pass/Permit/Fees: There is no admission to the Mμseum since the building is in the open.

Closest City or Town: Somerville

Physical Address:
The Mμseum (tiny museum)
71 Union Square #3032
Somerville, MA 02143

GPS Coordinates: 42.37986° N, 71.09490° W

Did You Know? The Mμseum name includes the Greek letter μ in its name. The letter is spelled out as *Mu*, and it's the twelfth letter of the Greek alphabet. Its scientific meaning is "micro," so the implied name is "micro museum."

Forest Park

Forest Park is one of the most historical portions of Springfield. The Victorian garden district is dominated by a park of the same name. The park is anchored by Porter Lake in the middle, and there are many athletic fields and courts throughout the area, along with a hockey arena, a small zoo, a rose garden, and America's first public swimming pool, opened in 1899. An 18-hole golf course is at the southeastern end.

The neighborhood itself houses some of the most historic homes in the commonwealth. Many were built from 1890 to 1910. Some of the homes feature Tudor Revival and Queen Anne designs.

Best Time to Visit: The park hosts a large light display every holiday season.

Pass/Permit/Fees: You can enjoy many activities around the park for free, but admission may be required for some indoor activities.

Closest City or Town: Springfield

Physical Address:
Forest Park
200 Tafton Rd
Springfield, MA 01108

GPS Coordinates: 42.07898° N, 72.56610° W

Did You Know? The X is the busiest part of the neighborhood. It is a commercial district named for the way the roads form an X shape.

Naismith Memorial Basketball Hall of Fame

The Naismith Memorial Basketball Hall of Fame in Springfield is dedicated to the sport of basketball and its evolution. The hall highlights the history of the sport and includes artifacts showcasing its origins in Springfield and how it has changed over the years. The Hall of Fame celebrates many of the sport's greatest icons. There are more than 400 inductees in the Hall of Fame, including players, coaches, and contributors to the sport.

Best Time to Visit: The Hall of Fame's annual induction ceremony is held every September.

Pass/Permit/Fees: Admission is $25.50 for adults and $16.50 for children.

Closest City or Town: Springfield

Physical Address:
Naismith Memorial Basketball Hall of Fame
1000 Hall of Fame Ave
Springfield, MA 01105

GPS Coordinates: 42.09403° N, 72.58504° W

Did You Know? James Naismith invented the sport of basketball in Springfield in December 1891. He created the game of "basketball," as it was originally called, by posting a peach basket above a door at one end of the Springfield College gymnasium and having players attempt to shoot a ball into the basket.

Paramount Theater

The Paramount Theater in Springfield is a historic building constructed in 1926 at the cost of over $1 million as part of the Massasoit House hotel. It has been used as a nightclub and concert venue, but most of the theater's history has been in movie screenings.

The theater includes an ornate series of murals inside. There are multiple tiers of seating, and the design is arranged so that all people will have a quality view without any obstructions. It has a capacity of 2,450 guests.

Best Time to Visit: The showings and events at the theater vary throughout the year.

Pass/Permit/Fees: The cost of admission will vary by event.

Closest City or Town: Springfield

Physical Address:
Paramount Theater
1676 Main St
Springfield, MA 01103

GPS Coordinates: 42.10459° N, 72.59478° W

Did You Know? The Paramount Theater was referred to as "the Hippodrome" for much of its life. The Hippodrome marquee is still outside the building.

Six Flags New England

Six Flags New England is an amusement park in the Springfield suburb of Agawam near the Connecticut border. The park, located on the west bank of the Connecticut River, has been open in some form since 1870. The park has more than 60 amusement rides, including 12 roller coasters. The Thunderbolt wooden coaster has been in operation since 1941. Newer coasters at the park include Batman: The Dark Knight and Superman the Ride, which travels up to 77 miles per hour and drops more than 200 feet. There are many games and dining spots and two separate areas for children at Kidzopolis and Looney Tunes Movie Town. The venue also has a water park called Six Flags Hurricane Harbor.

Best Time to Visit: The main park is open from April to September, with Hurricane Harbor open from June to August. The park hosts the Fright Fest event every October.

Pass/Permit/Fees: Admission prices vary by age and the date you visit. Prices range from $25 to $65 per person.

Closest City or Town: Springfield

Physical Address:
Six Flags New England
1623 Main St
Agawam, MA 01001

GPS Coordinates: 42.03823° N, 72.61350° W

Did You Know? The park was known as Riverside from 1887 to 1999. It was acquired by Six Flags and rebranded in 2000.

Springfield Armory National Historic Site

The Springfield Armory National Historical Site marks a manufacturing center for firearms for the American military that was active from 1777 to 1968. The armory is open for tours that will show you how many firearms and other military weapons were produced and how they evolved over the years.

The historic site features a thorough collection of firearms from over the years. It also includes exhibits about the many ways firearms have been used in military conflicts around the world.

Best Time to Visit: The site hosts various reenactments and outdoor events in the spring and summer.

Pass/Permit/Fees: The site is free to visit.

Closest City or Town: Springfield

Physical Address:
Springfield Armory National Historic Site
1 Armory St #2
Springfield, MA 01105

GPS Coordinates: 42.10740° N, 72.58155° W

Did You Know? During the Civil War, this Union armory produced firearms about 30 times faster than Confederate armories.

Norman Rockwell Museum

The Norman Rockwell Museum in Stockbridge features hundreds of original art pieces from the famed artist. The museum has many of his paintings, including some of the many covers he produced for the *Saturday Evening Post*.

Among the most famous works on display here include his Four Freedoms series, *No Swimming*, and *The Problem We All Live With*. Rockwell's art studio is next to the museum. It features many of his tools and materials.

Best Time to Visit: The museum often has special events taking place around Rockwell's birthday on February 3.

Pass/Permit/Fees: Admission is $20 for adults; $18 for seniors, AAA, and retired military; $15 for teachers (with valid MTA ID); and $10 for college students. Children 18 years and younger, active military, those with SNAP\EBT\Connector Cards, and front-line medical workers are all free.

Closest City or Town: Stockbridge

Physical Address:
Norman Rockwell Museum
9 Glendale Rd
Stockbridge, MA 01262

GPS Coordinates: 42.28777° N, 73.33574° W

Did You Know? Norman Rockwell lived in Stockbridge during the last few years of his life. He died in the town in 1978.

Gunn Brook Falls

Gunn Brook Falls in Sunderland is one of the most elaborate waterfalls in the commonwealth. Located in the Mount Toby State Forest, the waterfall consists of two portions: the Upper Falls, which is 15 feet high, and the Lower Falls, which is 10 feet high and a few feet narrower. The two waterfalls produce multiple cascades as the water flows.

The waterfall is on a short, 0.2-mile hiking trail in the northwestern part of the forest and forms from Gunn Brook, which comes from the Connecticut River to the west.

Best Time to Visit: The waterfall is more likely to be running in the spring because rainfall is more common during that season. It may be dried up during the summer or frozen over in the winter.

Pass/Permit/Fees: The waterfall is free to visit.

Closest City or Town: Sunderland

Physical Address:
Gunn Brook
Sunderland, MA 01375

GPS Coordinates: 42.49660° N, 72.55150° W

Did You Know? Part of the waterfall requires you to walk through the nearby water to see everything, although the water is shallow enough that you should only need wading shoes.

Purgatory Chasm State Reservation

Purgatory Chasm in Sutton is a geologic preserve that's about 70 feet deep and a quarter of a mile long. The chasm is shaped from granite that produces distinct ice patterns during the winter. Sometimes, the ice will stick around until the early part of the summer.

The chasm is believed to have been formed by glacial meltwater about 14,000 years ago. The meltwater came from an ice dam that tore out of the bedrock in the area.

You can see the chasm in the middle of Purgatory Chasm State Reservation. The area is operated by the Commonwealth of Massachusetts.

Best Time to Visit: The chasm is closed off during the winter months due to the ice hazard. Aim to visit during the summer or fall months if possible.

Pass/Permit/Fees: It's free to visit. You can go rock climbing in the area, but you'll require a permit to do so.

Closest City or Town: Sutton

Physical Address:
Purgatory Chasm State Reservation
198 Purgatory Rd
Sutton, MA 01590

GPS Coordinates: 42.12802° N, 71.71645° W

Did You Know? You will find about 2 miles of trail space around the chasm. Some of these spots may be closed off during the winter.

Lake Quannapowitt

Lake Quannapowitt is a lake in the Middlesex County town of Wakefield. Originally known as Reading Pond, it was renamed for Quonopohit, the Naumkeag Native American who signed a deed to the area that would become Wakefield in 1686. The lake is a prominent site for fishing because there are many warm-water fish species found throughout the area.

You can head out on the water at the Quannapowitt Yacht Club to the west. You'll see many beautiful trees and landscapes throughout the area while sailing here. The Lakewood Cemetery is to the southwest.

Best Time to Visit: The summer season is the most suitable time for sailing.

Pass/Permit/Fees: While you can reach the area for free, it may cost extra to reserve a time at the yacht club for using the boat ramp.

Closest City or Town: Wakefield

Physical Address:
Wakefield Farmers Market (on the Quannapowitt Lakeside)
468 North Ave
Wakefield, MA 01880

GPS Coordinates: 42.51442° N, 71.07810° W

Did You Know? Main Street in Wakefield goes along the eastern part of the lake. The area is popular for skating and walking.

Atlantic White Cedar Swamp Trail

The Atlantic White Cedar Swamp Trail is a mile-long trail near Wellfleet. Many lush trees surround the trail's wooden walkway. A large number of these trees and other parts of the swamp have been mostly undisturbed for more than 100 years.

You can see many oak and pine trees throughout the trail, which includes a boardwalk to White Cedar Swamp. A sandy road leads back to the start.

Best Time to Visit: The trail is easiest to traverse from April to October each year.

Pass/Permit/Fees: There's no fee to use the trail, but it is part of the Cape Cod National Seashore, and a $25 fee is charged for a vehicle to enter the area.

Closest City or Town: Wellfleet

Physical Address:
White Cedar Swamp Trail
Marconi Site Rd
South Wellfleet, MA 02663

GPS Coordinates: 41.91286° N, 69.97299° W

Did You Know? Some of the cliffs in the area are near the site of a wireless transmission station operated by Guglielmo Marconi in the early twentieth century. Some parts of the site have been preserved for viewing near the trail.

Horseneck Beach State Reservation

The Horseneck Beach State Reservation in Westport is a relaxing beach space in the southern part of the state near the Rhode Island border at the western end of Buzzards Bay. The reservation is on a peninsula that points toward the Rhode Island Sound.

The reservation has a ramp for boating and features walking and biking trails. The beach space is to the west and includes a few inland bodies of water surrounded by forested areas. There is also a campground on site with nearly a hundred camping spots available. Because of its ocean, beach, and estuary habitats, Horseneck is one of New England's best birding locations.

Best Time to Visit: The beach is open during most of the summer.

Pass/Permit/Fees: It costs $70 for non-residents to reserve a camping site. Commonwealth residents pay $22 instead.

Closest City or Town: Westport

Physical Address:
Horseneck Beach State Reservation
5 John Reed Rd
Westport, MA 02790

GPS Coordinates: 41.50909° N, 71.06387° W

Did You Know? The beach area used to have a few summer homes, but they were destroyed by hurricanes in 1938 and 1954. The land became a state-run beach afterward.

Woods Hole Science Aquarium

The aquarium features marine animals from the waters of the Northeastern and Mid-Atlantic United States. Indoor tanks and a touch tank display about 140 species of fish and invertebrates. An outdoor habitat provides a permanent home for injured seals.

The aquarium also operates a program to rehabilitate sea turtles that have washed up on Cape Cod beaches because they were injured or stunned by cold weather in late autumn. The turtles are rehabilitated until they are healthy enough to return to the wild, but they are not on public display.

Best Time to Visit: The aquarium is open daily except for federal holidays.

Pass/Permit/Fees: There is no admission charge.

Closest City or Town: Woods Hole

Physical Address:
Woods Hole Science Aquarium
166 Water St
Woods Hole, MA 02543

GPS Coordinates: 41.52678° N, 70.67399° W

Did You Know? Founded in 1885, this is the country's oldest public aquarium. Owned by the U.S. government, it is operated by the National Marine Fisheries Service and the Marine Biological Laboratory.

American Antiquarian Society

The American Antiquarian Society (AAS) in Worcester is the country's oldest historical society. The group focuses on the study of early American history. Founded in 1812, the AAS has a collection featuring millions of books and manuscripts relating to the history of the continent, the colonies, and the country. Some of the printed materials date back to the 1640s, when the first press was developed in the country.

Best Time to Visit: The AAS is open to visitors throughout the year.

Pass/Permit/Fees: While it is free to enter the space, you'll need to schedule an appointment to visit the AAS on weekdays. You'll also have to provide information on what you wish to look for while at the AAS site.

Closest City or Town: Worcester

Physical Address:
American Antiquarian Society
185 Salisbury St
Worcester, MA 01609

GPS Coordinates: 42.27739° N, 71.81018° W

Did You Know? Many prominent politicians have belonged to the AAS over the years, including John Adams, Andrew Jackson, Thomas Jefferson, James Monroe, and Franklin and Theodore Roosevelt.

EcoTarium

This science museum was founded in 1825 as the Worcester Lyceum of Natural History. In 1971, the museum moved into a new building and was renamed the Worcester Science Center. It became the New England Science Center in 1986 and the EcoTarium in 1998. Among the permanent exhibits are *The Arctic Next Door: Mount Washington*, which has many interactive displays and activity stations; *Nature Explore Outdoor*, which features numerous themed areas designed to interest children and their families through a variety of activities; *City Science: The Science You Live*; *Preschool Discovery Area*; *Secrets of the Forest*; and numerous outdoor living wildlife exhibits.

Best Time to Visit: Various traveling exhibits come to EcoTarium throughout the year. Visit the EcoTarium website for details.

Pass/Permit/Fees: Admission is $19 for adults and $14 for children.

Closest City or Town: Worcester

Physical Address:
EcoTarium
222 Harrington Way
Worcester, MA 01604

GPS Coordinates: 42.26451° N, 71.76932° W

Did You Know? The EcoTarium has a digital planetarium that offers many shows during the year, including ones that highlight astronomical features throughout the universe.

Elm Park

Elm Park in northwestern Worcester covers about 60 acres. The park has many walking paths and a pond crossed by two footbridges. Lincoln Pond takes up much of the space, and there are a few islands in the middle of the water.

The park has an ice-skating area that is open during the winter season. It also has a basketball court, a tennis court, a playground, and a few dog parks. There is even a disc golf course on the western end of the park.

Best Time to Visit: Many events are scheduled throughout the year, but most of them are conducted during the spring and summer.

Pass/Permit/Fees: You can visit Elm Park for free, but it may cost extra to reserve time on one of the athletic courts. Check the City of Worcester's website for details.

Closest City or Town: Worcester

Physical Address:
Elm Park
138 Russell St
Worcester, MA 01604

GPS Coordinates: 42.26831° N, 71.81644° W

Did You Know? Elm Park is one of the oldest municipal parks in the country. It was acquired by the city government in 1854.

Green Hill Park

Green Hill Park in Worcester has activities for the whole family to enjoy. The park has a petting zoo where children can see and pet various farm animals. There are also multiple athletic fields for baseball, soccer, and handball, plus a skate park. The 18-hole golf course to the north is open to the public. You can also fish in the pond in the middle of the park. The trails are surrounded by multiple types of trees. These include many native trees that were selected and planted by the City of Worcester, the park's operator.

Best Time to Visit: Watch for the trees as they change color during the fall.

Pass/Permit/Fees: While many of the features at the park are free, it does cost extra to reserve a tee time at the golf course. You can also rent some of the athletic fields for special events. Check with the park committee for details on what you might need to spend.

Closest City or Town: Worcester

Physical Address:
Green Hill Park
50 Skyline Dr
Worcester, MA 01605

GPS Coordinates: 42.28071° N, 71.77910° W

Did You Know? The 470-acre park is on space once owned by a local family. One family member dammed a nearby brook to form the pond in the middle of the park area in the eighteenth century.

Iris and B. Gerald Cantor Art Gallery

The College of the Holy Cross in Worcester is home to the Iris and B. Gerald Cantor Art Gallery. The museum focuses on the spiritual meanings of various art pieces. There are more than a thousand items in the museum's permanent collection.

You will find art pieces from many countries, including various abstract works from the United States. The museum is famous for its thorough array of Southeast Asian textiles. There are also collections of sculpture and photography.

Best Time to Visit: The gallery hosts many exhibitions throughout the year. Check with the museum for details on what exhibitions are available and what will be coming soon.

Pass/Permit/Fees: Admission to the museum is free.

Closest City or Town: Worcester

Physical Address:
College of the Holy Cross
1 College St
Worcester, MA 01610

GPS Coordinates: 42.23873° N, 71.80825° W

Did You Know? A recent major gift of drawings by American abstract expressionist Robert Beauchamp (1923–1995) was presented to the college by his widow, Nadine Valenti Beauchamp.

Mechanics Hall

Mechanics Hall is a concert venue in Worcester that opened in 1857 and was renovated in 1977. It is listed in the National Register of Historic Places. The Renaissance Revival building hosts many classical music performances throughout the year, and concerts for children and children's theater performances also take place.

The hall houses the Hook Organ. Installed in 1864, it features more than 3,500 pipes. It is one of the world's oldest four-keyboard organs in which the original configuration is preserved.

Best Time to Visit: The schedule at Mechanics Hall includes many shows each month, including a few Brown Bag Concerts held during lunch hours. Visit the Mechanics Hall website for details or to schedule a tour.

Pass/Permit/Fees: Ticket prices vary by event.

Closest City or Town: Worcester

Physical Address:
Mechanics Hall
321 Main St
Worcester, MA 01608

GPS Coordinates: 42.26556° N, 71.80052° W

Did You Know? Charles Dickens and Susan B. Anthony both spoke at the hall following its opening.

Salisbury Mansion

The Salisbury Mansion in Worcester was constructed in 1772 with an attached storehouse where Stephen Salisbury sold imported goods. In 1820, the store was closed, and the building became the Salisbury family residence until 1851. It has been restored to its condition as of the 1830s.

The mansion is two stories high with a framed body that includes flushboarded wood that was treated to look like stone. The home is available for tours. Many of the rooms have been furnished to reflect the proper time period.

Best Time to Visit: The museum is open for tours in the summer and fall.

Pass/Permit/Fees: Admission is $5.

Closest City or Town: Worcester

Physical Address:
Salisbury Mansion
40 Highland St
Worcester, MA 01609

GPS Coordinates: 42.27215° N, 71.80235° W

Did You Know? Historical records state that Stephen Salisbury was a "gentleman-merchant."

The Hanover Theatre for the Performing Arts

The Hanover Theatre for the Performing Arts in Worcester opened in 1904 and was rebuilt in 2008. The theater site was used as a vaudeville and burlesque venue and eventually became a silent-film theater. The venue made the transition to sound in the 1920s and continues to host various performances. The venue was shuttered for a few years but reopened in 2008, with the original entrance still standing to the side. The theater hosts many concerts and stage performance events, including touring Broadway shows.

Best Time to Visit: The theater's schedule changes throughout the year, so visit the theater's website for details on what shows are coming.

Pass/Permit/Fees: Ticket prices vary for each show at the theater.

Closest City or Town: Worcester

Physical Address:
The Hanover Theatre and Conservatory for the Performing Arts
2 Southbridge St
Worcester, MA 01608

GPS Coordinates: 42.26097° N, 71.80327° W

Did You Know? Theater magnate William Fox owned the venue for a brief time in the 1920s and 1930s. Fox-owned many movie palaces during that period.

The Sprinkler Factory

The industrial design of the Sprinkler Factory in Worcester is a small part of what makes this art studio interesting. It offers a thorough array of modern art pieces from many local artists.

The Sprinkler Factory houses original art pieces and sculptures with many unique themes. The gallery has a full schedule that highlights interesting events that make the site very popular among art enthusiasts throughout the Worcester area.

Best Time to Visit: The gallery hosts events during the year. Visit sprinklerfactory.com for details on what is happening here.

Pass/Permit/Fees: Admission prices vary depending on the specific event.

Closest City or Town: Worcester

Physical Address:
Sprinkler Factory
38 Harlow St
Worcester, MA 01605

GPS Coordinates: 42.28438° N, 71.79581° W

Did You Know? The Sprinkler Gallery is situated in the former home of the Rockwood Sprinkler Company, which was the first firm to produce industrial-sized automatic sprinkler systems.

Tuckerman Hall

One of the commonwealth's most historic concert halls is Tuckerman Hall in Worcester. Opened in 1902, it remains a popular site for events. Tuckerman Hall hosts weddings, corporate events, and many programs for nonprofit groups. The Massachusetts Symphony Orchestra also performs at the venue.

Tuckerman Hall displays several architectural influences. You will notice a mixture of Colonial Revival, Dutch, and Moorish influences in the structure.

Best Time to Visit: Tuckerman Hall hosts numerous events, but it is also interesting to look at from the outside. The unique architectural features of the building are accessible anytime in the year.

Pass/Permit/Fees: Admission varies by event.

Closest City or Town: Worcester

Physical Address:
Tuckerman Hall
10 Tuckerman St
Worcester, MA 01609

GPS Coordinates: 42.27351° N, 71.80124° W

Did You Know? Josephine Wright Chapman designed Tuckerman Hall for the Worcester Women's Club. Chapman was known for being one of the first women to work as a professional architect. She also designed Boston's New Century Building.

Worcester Historical Museum

Discover the history of Worcester at the Worcester Historical Museum, which hosts many artifacts and exhibits about the area's history. You will find items relating to the pre-colonial period of Massachusetts here. The venue also hosts many exciting exhibits illustrating points in Worcester's history.

The most popular exhibit at the museum is devoted to the development of the city. It includes exhibits on the people of Worcester and how they have helped make a positive impact on society.

Best Time to Visit: The museum has three main areas where various temporary exhibits are displayed. You can see what is playing on the museum's website.

Pass/Permit/Fees: Admission is $5.

Closest City or Town: Worcester

Physical Address:
Worcester Historical Museum
30 Elm St
Worcester, MA 01609

GPS Coordinates: 42.26500° N, 71.80443° W

Did You Know? The museum has been in operation since 1875. It was originally called the Worcester Society of Antiquity.

Proper Planning

With this guide, you are well on your way to properly planning a marvelous adventure. When you plan your travels, you should become familiar with the area, save any maps to your phone for access without internet, and bring plenty of water—especially during the summer months. Depending on which adventure you choose, you will also want to bring snacks or even a lunch. For younger children, you should do your research and find destinations that best suit your family's needs. You should also plan when and where to get gas, local lodgings, and food. We've done our best to group these destinations based on nearby towns and cities to help make planning easier.

Dangerous Wildlife

There are several dangerous animals and insects you may encounter while hiking. With a good dose of caution and awareness, you can explore safely. Here are steps you can take to keep yourself and your loved ones safe from dangerous flora and fauna while exploring:

- Keep to the established trails.
- Do not look under rocks, leaves, or sticks.
- Keep hands and feet out of small crawl spaces, bushes, covered areas, or crevices.
- Wear long sleeves and pants to keep arms and legs protected.
- Keep your distance should you encounter any dangerous wildlife or plants.

Limited Cell Service

Do not rely on cell service for navigation or emergencies. Always have a map with you and let someone know where you are and how long you intend to be gone, just in case.

First Aid Information

Always travel with a first aid kit in case of emergencies.

Here are items you should be certain to include in your primary first aid kit:

- Nitrile gloves
- Blister care products
- Band-Aids in multiple sizes and waterproof type
- Ace wrap and athletic tape
- Alcohol wipes and antibiotic ointment
- Irrigation syringe
- Tweezers, nail clippers, trauma shears, safety pins
- Small zip-lock bags containing contaminated trash

It is recommended to also keep a secondary first aid kit, especially when hiking, for more serious injuries or medical emergencies. Items in this should include:

- Blood clotting sponges
- Sterile gauze pads
- Trauma pads

- Second-skin/burn treatment
- Triangular bandages/sling
- Butterfly strips
- Tincture of benzoin
- Medications (ibuprofen, acetaminophen, antihistamine, aspirin, etc.)
- Thermometer
- CPR mask
- Wilderness medicine handbook
- Antivenin

There is much more to explore, but this is a great start.

For information on all national parks, visit https://www.nps.gov/index.htm .

This site will give you information on up-to-date entrance fees and how to purchase a park pass for unlimited access to national and state parks. This site will also introduce you to all of the trails at each park.

Always check before you travel to destinations to make sure there are no closures. Some hiking trails close when there is heavy rain or snow in the area and other parks close parts of their land for the migration of wildlife. Attractions may change their hours or temporarily shut down for various reasons. Check the websites for the most up-to-date information.